The Great Tradition—A Great Labor

The Great Tradition—A Great Labor

Studies in Ancient-Future Faith

EDITED BY
PHILIP HARROLD AND D. H. WILLIAMS

CASCADE *Books* • Eugene, Oregon

THE GREAT TRADITION—A GREAT LABOR
Studies in Ancient-Future Faith

Copyright © 2011 Wipf and Stock Publishers. All rights reserved. Except for brief quotations in critical publications or reviews, no part of this book may be reproduced in any manner without prior written permission from the publisher. Write: Permissions, Wipf and Stock Publishers, 199 W. 8th Ave., Suite 3, Eugene, OR 97401.

Cascade Books
An Imprint of Wipf and Stock Publishers
199 W. 8th Ave., Suite 3
Eugene, OR 97401

www.wipfandstock.com

ISBN 13: 978-1-60899-814-2

Cataloging-in-Publication data:

The great tradition—a great labor : studies in ancient-future faith / edited by D. H. Williams and Philip Harrold.

x + 114 p. ; 23 cm.

ISBN 13: 978-1-60899-814-2

1. Theology—History. I. Williams, Daniel H. II. Harrold, Philip. III. IV.

BT21.3 .G74 2011

Manufactured in the U.S.A.

This collection of essays is dedicated to

Andrew Walker

who was originally scheduled to speak at the Ancient Wisdom–Anglican Futures Conference (Trinity School for Ministry, Ambridge, Pennsylvania) in June of 2009 but was unable to attend due to a debilitating illness. Andrew is Professor of Theology and Education at King's College London. His contributions to, and editing (with Luke Bretherton) of, a collection of essays entitled *Remember Our Future: Explorations in Deep Church* (London: Paternoster, 2007) were a major inspiration for the conference. He is widely appreciated in the United Kingdom and the United States for reminding contemporary evangelicals of C. S. Lewis's appreciative inquiry concerning the common historical Christian tradition—"Deep Church." May this volume reflect the spiritual realities "down in the depths" of Christ's Church for the sake of witness and mission today and in the future.

Contents

List of Contributors | ix

Introduction by Philip Harrold | 1

ONE The Labor of Defining and Interpreting the Tradition | 9
D. H. Williams

TWO Authentic Participation in the Great Tradition | 25
Tony Clark

THREE Presumption, Preparation, *Parrēsia*, *Perichōrēsis*, and Worship | 38
Edith Humphrey

FOUR The Future of the Liturgy: A Pentecostal Contribution | 55
Simon Chan

FIVE Community: To What End? | 70
D. Stephen Long

SIX Apostolic Ministry Revisited | 81
George Sumner

SEVEN Emerging Church: A Victorian Prequel | 92
Dominic Erdozain

Contributors

Simon Chan is the Earnest Lau Professor of Systematic Theology at Trinity College (Lutheran), Singapore. Chan's most recent book is *Liturgical Theology: The Church as Worshipping Community* (Downers Grove: InterVarsity, 2006).

Tony Clark is Associate Professor of Ethics at Friends University, Wichita, Kansas. Clark is the author of *Divine Revelation and Human Practice: Responsive and Imaginative Participation* (Eugene, OR: Cascade, 2008).

Dominic Erdozain is Lecturer in the History of Christianity, King's College London. Erdozain's book, *The Problem of Pleasure: Religion, Recreation and Sport in Britain, 1850-1920*, is currently under review for publication.

Philip Harrold is Associate Professor of Church History, Trinity School for Ministry (Anglican), Ambridge, Pennsylvania. Harrold's most recent book is *A Place Somewhat Apart: The Private Worlds of a Late Nineteenth-Century Public University* (Eugene, OR: Pickwick, 2006).

Edith Humphrey is the William F. Orr Professor of New Testament at Pittsburgh Theological Seminary, Pittsburgh, Pennsylvania. Among Humphrey's recent books is *And I Turned to See the Voice: The Rhetoric of Vision in the New Testament* (Grand Rapids: Baker, 2007)

D. Stephen Long is Professor of Systematic Theology at Marquette University, Milwaukee, Wisconsin. Long's most recent book is *Speaking of God: Theology, Language, and Truth* (Grand Rapids: Eerdmans, 2008).

George Sumner is Principal and Helliwell Professor of World Mission at Wycliffe College, Toronto, Canada. Among Sumner's recent books is *Being Salt: A Theology of an Ordered Church* (Eugene, OR: Cascade, 2007).

D. H. Williams is Professor of Religion in Patristics and Historical Theology at Baylor University, Waco, Texas. William's recent books include *Tradition, Scripture and Interpretation: A Sourcebook of the Ancient Church* (Grand Rapids: Baker, 2006).

Introduction

Philip Harrold

What does it mean to inhabit the "Great Tradition" authentically? This question prompted a gathering called "Ancient Wisdom—Anglican Futures" at Trinity School for Ministry (Anglican), Ambridge, Pennsylvania in June of 2009. Based on their theological and liturgical catholicity and historic episcopate, Anglicans can be rather self-conscious about their "Great Tradition" status. But what the conference had to say about the Anglican tradition (with a small "t") applied to the Great Tradition (with a capital "T") as a whole. This is most apparent in the definition of *the* Tradition provided by theologian Daniel H. Williams: "The foundational legacy of apostolic and patristic faith, most accurately enshrined in Scripture and secondarily in the great confessions and creeds of the early church."[1]

One of the ways that Anglicans identify themselves is by appealing to universally recognized sources of the Christian faith rather than to particular doctrinal formulations. In the Chicago-Lambeth Quadrilateral (1888), for example, four articles are deemed necessary to a reunited Church: the Bible, the Creeds (Apostles and Nicene), and the Sacraments of Baptism and Holy Communion. The fourth touchstone is the historic episcopate, which is not so universally recognized but, nevertheless, gives

1. D. H. Williams, *Evangelicals and Tradition: The Formative Influence of the Early Church* (Grand Rapids: Baker, 2005) 24.

Anglicanism a distinctive link to the polity of the Eastern Orthodox and Roman Catholic churches. Even the distinctively Protestant flavor of the Anglican Articles of Religion (or Thirty-Nine Articles) is "born of an attempt (neither wholly successful nor wholly unsuccessful) to achieve comprehensiveness within the limits of a Christianity both catholic and reformed."[2] The *mere Christianity* represented by the Quadrilateral or the Articles inspires a great deal of reflection on what it means to be a historic church rooted in the canonicity and catholicity of Christian faith. It also brings Anglicans into dialogue with a resurgent *ressourcement* of the Great Tradition—what Robert Webber referred to some years ago as "ancient-future faith."

This volume of essays considers the possibility that the future of the Great Tradition in North America is not just about restoring or rebuilding something lost to the acids of modernity, the therapeutic amnesia of contemporary spirituality, or the pragmatism of entrepreneurial evangelicalism. These are pressing concerns, but the authors focus on what it means actually to receive and pass on the distinctive inheritance of historic Christianity for the sake of transformative worship, community, and mission in a postmodern world. They do so as theologians representing—or, at least, reflecting—Pentecostal, Baptist, Methodist, and Eastern Orthodox perspectives in varying degrees of dialogue with the Anglican tradition. In their different ways, the essays illustrate how bearing the Great Tradition is, to quote T. S. Eliot, a "great labour." It requires a kind of allegiance, vision, and praxis that is foreign to much of the contemporary evangelicalism which swells the ranks of those most eager to follow the Canterbury Trail.

For some time now, evangelicals in North America have been showing uncharacteristic interest in the history of the Church, especially in its ancient practices and enduring liturgical forms. The many works on spiritual disciplines by Richard Foster, stories of conversion to liturgical traditions by Peter Gillquist, Thomas Howard, and others, and Thomas Oden's prolific recovery of the early Fathers, are reactions to what J. I. Packer has called a "stunted ecclesiology," and John Stackhouse calls a "perpetual adolescence" in the subculture of evangelicalism. Writing in *Christianity Today* (February 2000), Chris Armstrong recalls that prior to his own journey into Anglicanism, "I felt like we were missing something

---

2. Oliver O'Donovan, *On the Thirty-Nine Articles: A Conversation with Tudor Christianity* (Exeter, UK: Paternoster, 1986) 12.

..." There was "no sense of the mystical massiveness of a church that had stood firmly for 2,000 years."

The late Robert Webber, himself an evangelical-turned-Anglican, was the most attuned to this angst and the most eager to nurture an "ancient-future" response. North American Anglicans have been the chief beneficiaries of his well-documented "Canterbury Trail" phenomenon, but at a particularly awkward time of tension and conflict in their history. The idea of an ancient-future is disorienting enough without being assimilated into a venerable tradition that has fast become unsure of its own pedigree. And what of the dizzying array of expectations that the so-called "younger evangelicals," in particular, bring with them? Included in their "profile" from Webber's book, *The Younger Evangelicals* (2002), are concerns as wide-ranging as how to live in a post-9/11 world, standing for "the absolutes of the Christian faith in a new way," communicating the faith "through stories" or "performative symbol," longing for "community," demanding "authenticity," and nurturing a "facility with technology."[3]

Can—or, perhaps, *ought*—the Great Tradition, whether refracted through the lens of Anglicanism or some wider field of vision, accommodate this profile? Given its long history of dynamic transmission of the faith once delivered to the saints, can the "foundational legacy of apostolic and patristic faith" be remixed with the wild imaginings of self-styled "emergents"? The conversionist activism of evangelicals? The deconversionist impulses of post-evangelicals? Will the "great convergence" of evangelical biblicism, charismatic experience, and liturgical practice produce a faithfulness that is both timeless and timely in an increasingly bewildering late-modern world?

Both participants in, and observers of, the so-called "emerging church" have highlighted a varied and, at times, bewildering movement of protest within the contemporary evangelical and post-evangelical world.[4] Self-styled "emergents" now speak of a more mature stage of

3. Robert E. Webber, *The Younger Evangelicals: Facing the Challenges of the New World* (Grand Rapids: Baker, 2002) 54.

4. Recent descriptions of emerging, emergent, and various dissenting movements, especially in contemporary evangelical Christianity, are found in Scot McKnight, "Five Streams of the Emerging Church," *Christianity Today* (February 2007) 35–39; "McLaren Emerging," *Christianity Today* (September 2008); and Phyllis Tickle, "The Great Emergence," *Sojourners* (August 2008). McKnight makes a distinction between *emergent*, as represented in Emergent Village and its leaders Brian McLaren, Tony Jones, and Doug Pagitt, and *emerging*, which is a "mix of orthodox, missional, evangelical, church-centered and social justice leaders and lay folk." Tickle uses *emergence* in a broad

critical self-awareness, focusing on internal problems like "institutional naivety" and "commodification" while celebrating a vibrancy of reflection on missiology, Christology, and ecclesiology. It has become more readily apparent to observers that a certain strand of the postmodern emerging church has begun to move in a premodern direction—perhaps the latest version of that late-twentieth-century phenomenon known as "the Canterbury Trail."

Robert Webber was not the first evangelical theologian to talk about postmodernity, but in 1999, he broke new ground when he linked the resources of the ancient Church to the sensibilities of postmodern people. It is important to note that Webber never capitulated to postmodern epistemology. He believed that the answer to the postmodern philosophical impasse was to be found in the ancient Christian faith with its strong emphasis on faith (the kind you stake your life on), taught, believed, and lived out in a community of commitment. Now, a decade later, elements of Webber's theological-cultural-liturgical-ecclesiological integration have flourished and become commonplace among evangelicals. Various academic and pastoral enterprises are now elaborating the ways that ancient faith can inform and renew evangelicalism. According to David Neff, another ten years will likely bring maturity to a number of these enterprises.[5]

Key to this maturity is recognition that genuine participation in the Great Tradition is hard work. Recalling T. S. Eliot's observation about how any valued and time-honored tradition can only be obtained by "great labour," Williams proposes that the next phase of evangelical *ressourcement* of the early Church must go beyond the current fascination with ancient liturgies and recitation of a few creeds. More precisely, evangelicals will need to engage the faith with a critical reception of the Church's dogmatic

---

historical sense for those movements within Christianity that, about every five hundred years, break through the institutional "carapace" of the Church "in order that renewal and new growth may occur." Included here is a diverse assortment of "young evangelicals," post-evangelicals and dissenting Catholics—all seeking "a new, more vital form of Christianity." At the "Ancient Wisdom—Anglican Futures" Conference, participants received introductory overviews of the *emergent* and *emerging* phenomena from Jason Clark (Co-ordinator for Emergent-UK) and Holly Rankin Zaher (Director of Student Discipleship, St. George's Episcopal Church, Nashville, Tennessee).

5. These observations are based on a presentation by David Neff (Editor in Chief and Vice President of Christianity Today Media Group) at the "Ancient Wisdom—Anglican Futures" Conference. He provided additional insights concerning the influence of Robert Webber on the "ancient-future" strand of the *emergent/emerging* movements.

inheritance; at least its doctrinal core, which is housed within confessional, apologetic writings, along with histories and biblical commentaries. If the early Church was grounded on theological issues deemed indispensible to the Christian identity, how can evangelicals appropriate the ancients without serious acknowledgment of this pattern? They will be able to do so only by nurturing a unique Christian culture that will have to interact with and yet withstand the intellectual winds of our time.

Tony Clark provides an illustration of how *not* to engage in the retrieval called for by Williams. In the first part of his paper, Clark reviews Phyllis Tickle's recent and widely read book, *The Great Emergence*. The book claims that the Church's history conforms to a pattern in which periods of struggle, arising every five hundred years, resolve in the emergence of a radically transformed church. There is some irony in the fact that Tickle's "emergent" appeal to a postmodern "rummage sale" in the Church relies heavily on a modern sense that history is guided by internal structures and mechanical processes that can be discerned objectively and predicted by the well-trained observer. Clark suggests otherwise. Rather than attempt to understand the Church and its emergence according to a grand scheme discerned from a detached perspective, a more authentic approach is one in which understanding arises from a deep and committed participation within the tradition. In making this claim, Clark shows that our knowledge of the tradition is rooted in the very practices that constitute it. Although we do articulate this knowledge in terms of creeds, confessions, etc. (an important practice in itself), there is much that we really know that we cannot tell.

Together, Williams and Clark remind us that the Great Tradition is carried along by two forms of knowing—one articulate, in the form of creeds, confessions, etc., and the other embodied or practical in nature. To participate in the Great Tradition means that we will indwell it through a wide array of practices that teach us the "grammar" of the faith. This happens as much through nurture and internalization as reflective endeavor, which brings us to the themes of worship, community, and mission.

Edith Humphrey draws on the experience of being overwhelmed or struck with wonder, and how readily this can be diminished in Christian worship. In varied ways, worshipers frequently approach the divine in terms of contract and exchange—perhaps as a pre-emptive move to mitigate their fear of the unknown. Alternately, others have thought it necessary to create drama in the worship-moment, as though it were necessary to amplify the significance of what is happening. The matter is complicated for many Western Christians, who continue in the Protestant tradition of reaction against a magical view of worship, but who yearn for awe and reverence in a world of instant yet shallow gratification. Humphrey's essay considers the clashing presuppositions concerning worship that make it difficult for those in the free-church tradition to understand the stance of humility in traditional Christian services. With the help of the Scriptures (Isaiah, 2 Corinthians, Hebrews, John, Revelation), and through examples from Western and Eastern liturgies, she considers the difference between presumption and Christian boldness (*parrēsia*), the necessity of continued preparation and penitence, and the astonishing hope that we may, in worship, reflect the perichoretic union of the Holy Trinity.

Certainly the ancient liturgies—from both East and West—offer strong Trinitarian foundations for Christian worship. That is why they are receiving more attention from evangelicals and Pentecostals who are attempting to recover what Simon Chan calls "*the* defining characteristic" of the Church. But this interest in early Christian worship is also bringing three streams together in a way that is *mutually* beneficial. The Great Tradition is not only received and passed-on but revitalized by what evangelicals and Pentecostals bring to the table. Chan draws attention to the possibility that an implicit Pentecostal sacramentality coupled with a practical doctrine of the Holy Spirit could greatly enrich what he perceives to be the pneumatologically deficient Western liturgical traditions, including the Anglican tradition. He shows how Pentecostals acknowledge, at least implicitly, the *epicletic* orientation of the Church in their emphasis on invocation of the Holy Spirit and the ministry of healing. They do so in a way that contrasts with the relatively subordinate role of the Spirit in the Western liturgies. Surely, Chan argues, the theology and practice of the Spirit witnessed in the Pentecostal stream can enrich the Great Tradition, ensuring that it will continue as a *living* tradition.

Just as Chan calls for a mutual exchange between the Great Tradition and contemporary Pentecostalism, D. Stephen Long points to a major contribution from historic evangelicalism that is often overlooked in today's ancient-future faith. He reminds us that the great eighteenth-century evangelist John Wesley understood the Great Tradition in profoundly "communal" terms. Wesley wrote, "I shall endeavor to show that Christianity is essentially a social religion, and that to turn it into a solitary relation is indeed to destroy it. . . . Secondly, that to conceal this religion is impossible." Wesley was no innovator in stating this. Instead, he drew on the historic faith in order to make two claims. First, Christianity is not about a solitary, individual relation with God, but can only rightly be understood as "communal." Second, the communal character of Christianity cannot but be a public witness. This is evangelism. Long explains both of these points, and in a case study, shows how Wesley's understanding of the communal character of Christianity can contribute to the vitality of a newly born liturgical community today.

The Great Tradition has little to say about community apart from the Church and, especially, the Church gathered around and defined by "apostolic ministry." George Sumner's paper turns to the subject of mission in light of this ministry. From Luke's account of the early Church in Acts, to the Northumbrian Church of the seventh century and Leslie Newbigin's revisioning of the episcopate in the founding of the Church of South India, we see a persistent interdependence between the strength and vitality of the Christian community and its apostolicity. Sumner underscores the dynamic relationship of charism to order and their convergences in some of the most pivotal moments of Church history. He also suggests how a renewed concept of apostolic leadership can be realized in the Great Tradition today.

Dominic Erdozain follows suit with a vivid history lesson from the English Victorians and, in doing so, ends where we began with an intersection between the Great Tradition and the emerging/emergence conversation. He argues that history can enrich contemporary debates on church, mission, and society by providing both a "vertical" dimension of contextualization and internal, "traditioned" resources for renewal. Erdozain's paper interprets the evangelical voluntarism of nineteenth-century Britain as a forerunner of the emerging church, highlighting creative appropriations from, as well as more precarious accommodations to, contemporary culture. While such pioneer ministries claim a just place within the Great Tradition, translating the gospel into a compelling vernacular, they also demonstrate the tendency of pragmatism, practicality, and specialization to "occlude" gospel imperatives—a process that presages what Andrew Walker and others have termed "gospel amnesia." Erdozain's presentation concludes with a discussion of the late-Victorian search for a more exalted ecclesiology—presaging, perhaps, the more recent search for an evangelical doctrine of the Church.

These papers demonstrate the growing importance of the Great Tradition within a broad spectrum of contemporary evangelical, Pentecostal, and, yes, emergent faith. *What does it mean to inhabit the "Great Tradition" authentically?* The convergences are interesting in themselves—certainly key to the highly dynamic transmission process that characterizes any living tradition, capital "T" or small "t." But also of interest are the negotiations that make these convergences possible. The contributions to this volume show how "profitable and commodious" (borrowing from Richard Hooker) a Great Tradition can be in the worship, community, and mission of the Church in late modernity. If there is any lingering unease regarding the integrity and durability of the Great Tradition, perhaps it is to these lively elements that we should turn for deep insight and, borrowing from C. S. Lewis, "deep church." In this faithful witness, the ancient becomes future in God's mission to the world. Indeed, this is the great labor of the Great Tradition.

ONE

The Labor of Defining and Interpreting the Tradition

D. H. Williams

Now that the authority of the ancient church has become the rave of Evangelicals, the task of appropriating this authority for contemporary purposes has begun in earnest. There have been attempts to begin this task, as witnessed by the works of Thomas Oden, Robert Webber, and others, whose methods of retrieval entail a broad assumption that the patristic age was built and sustained on a theological continuum, best demonstrated by the great councils or theological texts. Oden has urged Evangelical readers to discover the "classic Christian consensual thinking," which he qualifies according to Vincent's canonical principle of orthodox faith: antiquity, universality, and consensus. Likewise, he has argued that theology needs to return to the orthodoxy or "classical Christianity," established by seven ecumenical councils and the eight great theologians, producing the Christian consensus of the first millennium.[1]

---

1. Thomas C. Oden, *The Living God*, vol. 1 of *Systematic Theology* (San Francisco: HarperCollins, 1987) ix–xv.

Other studies have been produced by Evangelicals based on the notion that early Christianity was essentially a unified movement in which orthodoxy and heresy were self-evident categories.[2] Indeed, the existence of historical continuity is part of the attraction for Free Church Protestants who seek to move beyond a heritage of theological and ecclesial fragmentation. Another example of this tendency is found in Robert Webber's *Ancient-Future Faith*, which explains how looking for unity "among believing Catholic, Orthodox, and Protestant Christians has taken me back to the common era, and to those convictions that *precede* a time when the church became *Eastern* Orthodox, *Roman* Catholic, or *Protestant*."[3] Webber is perhaps more guarded about matters of doctrinal accord, although, like Oden, he draws on Vincent's grand statement of catholic unity as a normative description of the early church.

At the same time there are just as important, more subtle, issues that must be considered for encountering the faith and life of the early church. Was there truly an ancient consensus historically speaking that is expressed in creeds or confessions of councils? Putting this in a more nuanced way: can we point to a sequence of events and writers within the early church that represented the catholic mainstream in faith and practice? Was the message of the Christian faith in the first five centuries sufficiently unified that there indeed existed an identifiable "mere Christianity"?

These questions are not merely academic, nor are they new. Over the last generation, patristic scholarship—both Protestant and Roman Catholic[4]—has generally *not* operated on the view that the accounts of

---

2. Christopher A. Hall, *Learning Theology with the Church Fathers* (Downers Grove: InterVarsity, 2002) 21. Hall writes: "whatever a father says in his teaching must be 'orthodox' or in line with what the apostles themselves [sic] taught and modeled." Little time is given to the idea that what counts as "orthodox" may change over time or may simply not be very clear. He likewise claims that Origen and others failed to receive the distinction of church father "because their positions drifted beyond the bounds of orthodoxy."

3. Robert E. Webber, *Ancient-Future Faith: Rethinking Evangelicalism for a Postmodern World* (Grand Rapids: Baker, 1999) 29.

4. For a contrast among Roman Catholic writers, see Adalbert Hamman, *How to Read the Church Fathers* (Chestnut Ridge, NY: Crossroad, 1993): "A look back at the patristic period shows clearly enough that here we have fully developed thought, implemented in action, by responsible pastors of churches" (123), and Terrence Tilley, *Inventing Catholic Tradition* (Maryknoll, NY: Orbis, 2000), a Roman Catholic theologian, who claims the beliefs and practices deemed as "traditional" by the Church hierarchy are not found in the previous ages of the church, either in their present form or have no precedent at all because beliefs and practices are always in motion and therefore changing.

"orthodox" church history[5] accurately represent the voices of historic catholicism. This means that earliest Christianity was not, as Tertullian once declared, "a body woven together by a common religious profession, and by the unity of discipline."[6] On the basis of historical-contextual interpretations, the conclusion is more commonly drawn that multiplicity and religious plurality was from the beginning, which runs into the teeth of a broad consensual construal of apostolic and patristic Christianity.

The Word Made Flesh: A History of Christian Thought by Margaret Miles articulates a familiar approach when she discusses methodology. "If history should deliver a 'story,' whose story should be told, whose perspective represented?" The "new historicism," as Miles calls it, does "not fit or support the 'great story'" and "challenge[s] the illusion that the past can be packaged as a coherent narrative." As a result, "Christian ideas and practices across the centuries of the common era had little uniformity. Thus, historical Christianity should not be studied with the goal of identifying the historical antecedents of present values, ideas, beliefs, and practices though this has frequently been done."[7]

Another sketch of Christian history, by Mark Humphries, this one focused on the patristic period, argues that the designation "church fathers" is "quite arbitrary and unsubtle."[8] He rejects the propensity among Christians to find some form of a "golden age" that is somehow "pure and free from corruption" since it was a characteristic of early church writers to stress the essential unity of the Christian movement.[9] It is unclear whether Humphries is warning the reader against embracing facile interpretations of the church's ancient past or that any form of theological or ecclesiastical unity is a chimera.

In the preface of his book, *Lost Christianities*, Bart Ehrman makes the startling comment, "During the first three centuries, the practices and beliefs found among people who called themselves Christian were so varied that the differences between Roman Catholics, Primitive Baptists

---

5. Such as Eusebius, *Historia ecclesiastica* (c. 300 CE), or Rufinus' Latin continuation of Eusebius' work (c. 404) that goes by the same name.

6. *Apologeticum* 39.

7. Margaret R. Miles, *The Word Made Flesh: A History of Christian Thought* (Oxford: Blackwell, 2005) 7.

8. Mark Humphries, *Early Christianity* (London: Routledge, 2007) 76.

9. Ibid., 147.

and Seventh Day Adventists pale by comparison."[10] To speak seriously about a proto-orthodox Christianity, *as Ehrman himself once did*, can no longer be squared with the historical multiplicity of various canonical lists of Scriptures nor with the plurality of Christian churches all claiming to be apostolic.

For Elaine Pagels and Karen King, the traditional history of Christianity is written from the viewpoint of the victors, who "were remarkably successful in silencing or distorting other voices."[11] Readers of Christian history will have heard this kind of stale and hackneyed argument many times before. By "other voices," Pagels and King of course mean whatever group of Gnostic Christians produced the gospel of Judas. Were it not for the circumstantial discovery of these sources of dissent, we should never know about the "extraordinarily dynamic world in which Christianity was shaped," that now challenges us "to see with new eyes the familiar traditions we call Christianity."[12] There is no subtlety or nuance in their assertion here that the kind of Christianity called orthodox actively sought to undermine the truth of its contemporaries.

Judging from the conclusions of these recent writers, which continue to inform broad assumptions in historical theology, it would seem that "retrieving" or "recovering" classical Christianity can be done only by committing violence to the unique and multiform character of its earliest centuries. "Consensual Christianity" is a dogmatic illusion that demands contemporary correction. Moreover, the ancient conflict between a Christian "orthodoxy" and other Christian systems has now been reinterpreted in terms of ecclesial struggle for power. Theology functions more as a pretext for deeper formative political processes working within churches. This aspect of Walter Bauer's theory about doctrinal dispute in earliest Christianity is still very much alive.[13] One result of this approach is that the very notion of "orthodoxy" breeds a historical triumphalism or arrogance that should be avoided at all costs.

Coming at the matter from the other direction, I have wondered whether enough present-day Evangelicals, in their fervor to identify

---

10. Bart Ehrman, *Lost Christianities* (Oxford: Oxford University Press, 2003) 1.

11. Elaine Pagels and Karen King, *Reading Judas: The Gospel of Judas and Shaping of Christianity* (New York: Viking, 2007) xviii.

12. Ibid., xxii.

13. See, especially, Walter Bauer, *Orthodoxy and Heresy in Earliest Christianity* (Minneapolis: Fortress, 1971).

themselves with the life and thought of the ancient church, are aware of the great and precarious balancing act that produced what we call orthodoxy. Like Scripture, the early tradition did not merely fall down from heaven into the hands of the faithful, but was constructed—even if providentially—over time. A populist recovery or retrieval of patristic Christianity emphasizes discovering or creating a unified narrative that ploughs its way through the warp and woof of church history regardless of the complications. This tendency places a focus on the ends, not the means. We want to know simply what the early church taught about a particular subject, or what a council decreed, or who the orthodox were and who the heretics were.

Working from this platform we may find it easier to use brief extracts in translation from the ancients than it is to study them directly *in extenso*. While there is nothing necessarily wrong with this approach—this was how Christian learning was achieved for most of the medieval era—it may betray an impatience that prefers the most expedient route of determining the "message" of the ancient churches. The most obvious problem with this practice is that the patristic texts become decontextualized and thus subject to whatever historical pattern we wish to give them. Moreover, contemporary readers will inevitably become limited to the secondary interpretations given to the Fathers by modern writers. Is it any wonder that the *Da Vinci Code* was regarded as more than a piece of religious fiction?

While doctrinal theology is certainly not the only approach within patristic studies, the reality is that the study of doctrine has been assigned to an ephemeral place among the preferred methods of theologians and historians today. Part of the problem is that those who are carefully trained within the humanities have become sensitized, too often intimidated, by forces within the academy that no longer acknowledge the value of doctrinal matters (or almost any form of Christian preservationism or conservatism) as a legitimate way to "map" the course of historical Christianity.[14] Cultural contextualization is now the *right password*; it is the primary—sometimes only—concern of the serious scholar. Because dogmatic assertions, as one finds in ancient Christian texts, are derived from

---

14. Mark Lilla, "Taking the Right Seriously, " *The Chronicle of Higher Education* (Sept. 11, 2009). Lilla observes: "There is a concerted effort to keep conservative PhDs out of jobs, to deny tenure to those who get through, and to ignore conservative books and ideas" although this is "now instinctive and habitual rather than self-conscious, reflecting intellectual provincialism more than ideological fervor."

diverse contexts and multiple groups within specific cultural settings, it is not feasible to embrace a single voice that speaks for Christianity, much less work with fixed categories such as "orthodoxy" and "heresy." We are taught to content ourselves with the study of "method" and to avoid the pitfalls of interacting with the content of authoritative declarations that are found in our ancient texts.

While it is true that "orthodoxy" and "heresy" (and their implications) have been bandied about with little thought, still, moving to an opposite extreme is not a solution. To put it more plainly: just because Vincent exaggerated the Christian consensus does not mean we must consign ourselves to viewing all of Christian antiquity as a "bewildering mass of alternatives."[15] Why remove one kind of simplification only to replace it with another?

In point of fact, patristic specialists have long debated over how to describe both continuity and division within history, as well as how we should gauge the distinction between genuine developments from theological movements that ultimately become regarded as outside the catholic mainstream. Jaroslav Pelikan, R. P. C. Hanson, and Henry Chadwick, among others, have suggested ways for preserving the prerogative of finding diachronic streams of basic theological principles within the early church.[16] But their work has by no means solved all the problems entailed within doctrinal development within historic Christianity. Indeed, there is no one model that can comprehensively account for all the variables. Chadwick suggested that orthodoxy and heresy are related analogously to the comparison of a circle and an ellipse. Having different contours, the two do not fill the same area, yet there is a goodly amount of overlap between them—in this case, a doctrinal overlap that most Christians shared about fundamental or core truths about God, Christ, creation, and redemption. One thinks of the rule of faith or the multiple versions of the Apostles' Creed as embodying these core principles while at the same time allowing for an elasticity of expression and concept that always prompted the work of interpretation.

15. A description that Rodney Stark aptly used for defining ancient Paganism. See *The Rise of Christianity: A Sociologist Reconsiders History* (Princeton, NJ: Princeton University Press, 1996) 197.

16. If we doubt that there was disagreement or dissonance between the ancient thinkers, then we should consider a key witness to these discordances: the medieval scholastic exercises in dialectic that sought at great length and energy to reconcile patristic authorities.

I do not pretend to have the decisive word on exactly how Christian diversity and unity operated at the same time in the same places. It is undeniable, for instance, that different kinds of Gnosticisms flourished in Lyons where Irenaeus became bishop (c. 180), or that Montanism spread rapidly and widely within churches, initially being regarded as entirely catholic, or that Marcion's conclusions about the disparity between the old and new covenants enjoyed a high level of acceptance in both east and west well into the fifth century, or that monarchian explanations about the Father and Son as one God evolved in Rome, Carthage, and western Asia Minor as a functional theology among many Christian intellectuals. The task of defining and articulating the catholic faith was a messy business—a task that had always taken place amidst the clamor of alternative systems. There was nothing wholly abstract in this process; that is, doctrinal development always took place within the dynamics of the church communities that embraced doctrines and observed Christian practices.

If we try our best to let the ancient evidence speak for itself, we can drop the misguided notion that the second-century church understood the Father, Son, and Spirit in the same way as the fourth- and fifth-century theologians, or conversely, that Tertullian or Origen were "subordinationists" because they were not informed by the Nicene Creed. All of this must be distinguished from the meanings or significance we attribute to the so-called patristic "consensual understanding." Surely the Tradition was a matter of both *continuity* and *change*, of *fluid* and *fixed* elements (borrowing from H. E. W. Turner's definition). As such, doctrinal development proceeds on the basis of the Tradition's past that leads to revisions or qualifications of that past in the present. This is the very reason why there exist so many ecclesiastical creeds before the sixth century; this is why the Nicene Creed was qualified by the Constantinopolitan and Chalcedonian councils, yet both of which stoutly argued they were following Nicaea. These statements of faith are, in effect, milestones of the Tradition's argument with itself about the nature of orthodoxy as new doctrinal issues had to be addressed in light of what the church had believed. As the faith was *de facto* a reflection of the believing church—like a living language—so it would always be in a certain sense an internal process of progression in understanding and expression.

All this is to say that orthodox "solutions" are no more valuable for us today than *how* the church arrived at its orthodox solutions. In large part this will mean that Christians of all communions must not avoid doctrine and its development. Herein lies the problem, however. If there is one unspoken and central feature to the method of today's scholarly assessments of the past, it is that doctrine *divides*, whereas practice *unites*. This is the central lesson derived from the twentieth-century ecumenical movements from the World Council of Churches. With a few notable exceptions,[17] the ecumenism of that era predicated its efforts on this implicit thesis, namely, that ecclesial activity and liturgies offer greater possibility for cooperation than historical teaching. Since then this thesis has taken various incarnations in theological dialogue and debate, resulting (intentionally or not) in marginalizing doctrinal theology as providing a basis for unity.

Higher education within Roman Catholic universities is also reaping the whirlwind of having shunned dogmatics for the seemingly more benign sanctuaries of social justice and cultural diversity. The reception of *Ex corde ecclesiae* for the majority of Roman Catholic theologians in the United States has been so problematic that a large number of Catholic universities have either ignored it as too invasive of the more sacred principle of academic freedom, or have transformed the *mandatum*—constructed on the idea that Catholic theologians are accountable to the Church—into an entirely personal matter.[18] As a result, a small number of Catholic institutions of higher learning in the U.S. are unlikely to remain distinctively and recognizably Catholic."[19]

In sum, let me offer two preliminary observations:

1) Early Christian diversity, with its variables of context, faith, and views of succession, was real and undeniable. It was not, however, antagonistic in every location to a unifying core; nor does such variability naturally lead one to the posture of characterizing the catholic tradition as an oppressive force—a compelling of unity—that overcame all rivals.

---

17. Faith and Order conferences (of the World Council of Churches) held in Lund, Sweden (1952), Montreal (1963) and Lima, Peru (1982).

18. J. Augustine DiNoia, "Communion and the Ecclesial Vocation of the Theologian in Catholic Higher Education," in *The Enduring Nature of the Catholic University* (Manassas, VA: The Cardinal Newman Society, 2009) 51: "For one thing, that the vocation of theologians is a properly ecclesial one has been and continues to be doubted, disputed, or denied. Even if it is conceded that the theological profession entails a calling of some kind, it is supposed that this would be primarily an academic or intellectual vocation, involving overriding allegiances, not to a church or denomination, but to one's scholarly guild and the larger academic community."

19. Ibid., 56.

Contemporary writers err when they stress only the pluralist and multiform character of ancient Christianity, negating the possibility of a nucleus, whether dogmatic or liturgical, within the churches. The question, rather, is how rhetorically orchestrated were the early Christian claims for unity or for orthodoxy such that they ought to be construed as a form of religious propaganda or just fanciful thinking.

2) On the other hand, the search for a singular narrative of orthodoxy is too naïve and romantic a way of interpreting the early church. One can hope that there will be in the next phase of patristic *ressourcement* among Protestants a greater awareness of the ancient Christian tradition as it evolved through its struggles of self-definition and confessional division; an ongoing communitarian movement that experienced the ups and downs in the long process of theological consolidation. Generally speaking, it is time for Evangelicals to move from an idealist fascination with the early Fathers to a purposeful study and realization of the complexities involved when determining a course of doctrinal continuity within Christian antiquity.

A response to the atomizers of the patristic past calls for much more than louder reassertions of the ancients' broad consensus or of the value of pre-enlightenment exegesis. The French Roman Catholic *ressourcement* of the twentieth century does well to remind us that appropriating the ancients is not a simple turning to or repristination of the past. Retrieving the early Fathers was a matter of penetrating "to the vital source of their spirit . . . a spiritual and intellectual communion with Christianity . . . transmitted to us through its classic texts, a communion which would nourish, invigorate and rejuvenate" the present.[20] No one can deny that ancient texts—however diverse—secured a sufficient theological unity and definitive authority for all subsequent teaching and life within Christian churches.

If we wish to glean from and participate in the early church's life, it should entail our participation in their rough and tumble world of doctrinal definition and preservation given theological issues that they faced. However, it takes much time and effort to enter into this world and share in their vision. Thus I want to borrow from T. S. Eliot his characterization of tradition as a "labour." To quote him directly,

---

20. M. D'Ambrosio, "Ressourcement Theology, Aggiornamento, and the Hermeneutics of Tradition," *Communio* 18 (1991) 530–55.

> We have seen many such simple currents soon lost in the sand; and novelty is better than repetition. Tradition [however] is a matter of much wider significance. It cannot be inherited, and if you want it, you must obtain it by great labour.[21]

For present purposes, I will interpret this "labour" as the task of circumscribing and interpreting the ancient tradition that includes but must go beyond the current attraction to the liturgies, to the church calendar, or to scriptural exegesis. More precisely, our labor is necessary for a critical reception to the church's dogmatic inheritance—at least of its doctrinal core. As Benedict XVI has stated when he was Cardinal Ratzinger, "Dogma was conceived, not as an external shackle, but as the living source that made knowledge of the truth possible in the first place. The church came to life for us above all in the liturgy and in the great richness of the theological tradition."[22] This is an important and relevant admonition. Balanced scholarship or pastoral leadership must not be redirected by current pressures that avoid or annul the place of doctrine in favor of practice.[23] In the process of looking for ecclesial direction, we must beware of the prevalent temptation to reduce tradition to moral or liturgical practices as the means of finding a common denominator. Nor need we submit to the fragmentary approach toward early church history in such a way that even a circumspectly crafted doctrinal continuity is made impossible. However important it is to take into account the historical context of Christian antiquity, it is not a warrant for arresting the church's ability to discover those points of doctrinal or confessional development in its history.

I would like to spend the second half of this chapter addressing what assumptions we can make when referring to the early Fathers who received and handed over Christian doctrine. If we wish to learn something about the early church, both purposefulness and responsibility are called for as we seek to access the ancient Tradition.

First, it is debatable whether Christian doctrine or tradition was ever perceived in the static and immutable way as the naysayers have char-

---

21. T. S. Eliot, "Tradition and the Individual Talent," in *The Sacred Wood: Essays on Poetry and Criticism* (London: Methune, 1920) 26.

22. Cited in Joseph A. Komonchak, "The Church in Crisis: Pope Benedict's Theological Vision," *Commonweal* 132 (2005) 11.

23. An informed examination of unifying strands within ancient practices is itself a challenge as exhibited in Andrew Louth, "Unity and Diversity in the Fourth Century Church," in *Doctrinal Diversity: Varieties of Early Christianity*, ed. E. Ferguson, vol. 4 of *Recent Studies in Early Christianity* (New York: Garland, 1999) 11.

acterized it. So too, the scope of ancient catholicism's insistence for orthodox teaching and practice reveals something that is not a monolithic composition. During the earliest centuries of Christianity, we might say there were two sides to the *traditio: the outward and the inward*. The first seeks to define and preserve the Tradition in a linear and unchanging way, whereas the second, often intra-ecclesial, admits to the existence of a certain fringe or "loose ends" of what is taught and believed. This is the *sic et non* of early Christianity. While the rhetoric of these two approaches to tradition impacted each other and is not always this straightforward, they can be distinguished in the primary literature.

Let me try to demonstrate this distinction. According to Origen (mid third century), a common deterrent to Christianity was articulated by the Pagan intellectual Celsus who (Origen says) "reproaches us, by saying, 'Having grown in numbers and being widely dispersed, they are further split and divided; every body wants to have his own party.'"[24] In response, Origen does not argue against the division among Christians, but he asserts that they are not divided on important issues that lie at the center of the faith:

> In reply, we will say that you never find different sects in any department of thought unless the principle involved is one of grave importance and practical use. Take the science of Medicine. It is useful and necessary to the human race, and the questions which arise as to the healing of the body are many. . . . So too, many of the literary class were anxious to understand the meaning of Christianity. In consequence of this, because scholars differently interpreted what were believed on all sides to be Divine utterances, sects sprang up bearing the names of thinkers who had a reverent regard for the origin of the Word.[25]

When writing didactically about the church's teaching, Origen will likewise admit that Christians are not agreed on all important theological issues, but they are held together by what he calls "a definite limit and to lay down an unmistakable rule" (or "canon"), "clearly delivered in the teaching of the apostles."[26] Here Origen unfolds the basic elements of this canon. Undoubtedly, he is setting forth a version of the Rule of the Faith as known to him and his readers in Alexandria. As a philosopher and

24. *Against Celsus* III.12.
25. Ibid.
26. *On First Principles* I.2.

former catechist, Origen would have been quite familiar with where the "fixed and fluid" elements lay. Most importantly, there would have been absolutely no benefit in sustaining his case had Origen exaggerated or distorted the circumstances of the Christian Church.

The rule of faith, incidentally, is another instance of Christian unity within its diversity. Were one to comb through all the patristic sources, you would never find an *Ur-text* known as the Rule of Faith. Nor was the Rule as static or fixed as the early apologists might have us believe since we possess only variations of the Rule. They are hardly identical, and it is obvious that the appearance of each one possesses a particular context of language, location, and time that affected the teller's description of the Rule. But it is also obvious that there is pattern to these recitations that continued to reflect that association of bipartite and triadic confessional patterns found in the New Testament. Neither a fixed formula nor a mere listing of proof texts, these "Rules" manifest an oral traditional account of the church's preaching and teaching.[27]

Yet another instance of the church's theological *sic et non* is found in the mid-fourth century with the literary works of Hilary, bishop of Poitiers until *circa* 367. It is generally acknowledged that the majority of western bishops knew little or nothing about the Nicene Creed until the early 360s. Hilary was no exception. Not until the period of his eastern exile (356–360) did he become acquainted with the wording and potential value of the Creed as a unique expression of orthodoxy. As it was for most Latin speakers, the definition of Nicaea remained in subservience to the confession of faith by which Hilary was baptized.[28] But the ecclesial world became a bigger and more complicated place during this bishop's exile in the east. After four years of traveling around Asia Minor, he learned quite a bit about Greek theologies and creeds (including Nicaea) attributed to the councils of Antioch 341, of Sirmium 351, as well as the notorious creedal manifesto also issued from Sirmium of 357, which called for the rejection of any confession that contains *ousia* or substance language. The Sirmium formula also asserted that because the Son is begotten, the Father must be greater.[29]

---

27. R. P. C. Hanson, *Tradition in the Early Church* (Philadelphia: Westminster, 1962) 93.

28. Hilary *On the Trinity* XII.57: "Preserve O Lord, my pious faith undefiled . . . so that I may ever hold fast that which I professed in the creed of my regeneration when I was baptized in the Father, and the Son, and the Holy Spirit."

29. *On the Synods* 11.

Like a line of trenches established to confront the enemy, Hilary describes a pro-Nicene perspective of the Father and Son throughout *On the Trinity*,[30] a long document he began writing in exile. In Books II–III, written first, Hilary articulates the "dangerous errors" of those who insist that the Son was "produced out of nothing and in time" even though Scripture names Him "Image, Wisdom and Power of God" (1 Cor 2). They teach this, Hilary claims, in order to save God from being lowered to the Son's level as one who was born. By doing so, we are told, "they break up the absolute unity of God by assigning differences in nature" which is nothing less than destroying "the consistency and totality of the mystery of faith."[31]

About the same year that Hilary wrote these words, he also sent a letter to his fellow bishops in Gaul in response to their request for information about eastern confessions of faith. When he came to discussing *homoousios*, Hilary qualifies it as potentially teaching a monarchial view of God, and that eastern bishops were not completely wrong to have suspicions about the Nicene word. In fact, the recent Greek reference to the Son as "similar in essence" (*homoiousios*) to the Father may be used just as piously as Nicaea when it comes to expressing their relation. Even more striking, Hilary presents positive comments on the Sirmium Creed of 351, *contra* the opinion of Athanasius who said it was another ploy of the "Arians."[32] A case in point is that the creed of (the council of) 351 anathematized anyone who claims the Father and the Son are two gods with the reason that "the Son is not equal or the peer of the Father, but [we] understand the Son to be subject."[33] Although this view was rank heresy for Athanasius, Hilary interprets this statement for his Gallic brethren not as obviously subordinationist; rather, it was the council's way of preserving a true distinction between Father and Son against modalist exegesis.

Well over two centuries following Irenaeus' observations about the church's geographically diffuse but generally unified nature, Augustine says something very similar:

---

30. It is very much in keeping with the wording of Nicaea that Hilary says little about the Holy Spirit. The work was probably originally entitled *De fide*, and it appears that it was originally written as two separate works later joined together. See Carl Beckwith, *Hilary of Poitiers on the Trinity* (Oxford: Oxford University Press, 2008) chapters 4–6.

31. *On the Trinity* II.4.

32. *On the Synods* 26.

33. *On the Synods* 50.

> The Catholic Church, spread over the length and breadth of the whole world, has turned back these assaults of earlier times [namely, "heretics who look for glory"] and has become increasingly stronger—not by resistance but by patient endurance.... It is not troubled by the charge of harboring unworthy members since it is on its guard to distinguish carefully between the harvest season, the threshing season, and the storage season.[34]

Augustine acknowledged theological discord within the catholicism of his day; indeed, he was only too well aware that the Donatists constituted the majority of Christians in Hippo Regius. His intended readership—a more general audience than many of his other works—would have also been acquainted with those who defined themselves as another kind of catholic. In fact, the point of Augustine's writing was to make careful distinctions between the catholicism he defended and that of his opponents, since the amount of overlap between doctrinal issues was significant enough to be confusing to the unschooled.

It may sound odd, but it is remarkable that writers in the late-fourth and fifth centuries *did not* censure many more pre-Nicene writers than they did. And in the few cases of post-mortem condemnations, such as Tertullian and Origen, the reasons were not based on Christological or Trinitarian theology, even though Tertullian and Origen refer to God the Son as "second" to the Father. Justin's and Irenaeus' interpretation of Christ's suffering in the Garden was grounded on their opposition to any Gnostic or docetic view; Christ was the Father's *logos* who was made flesh, truly suffering and assuming our very weaknesses in every way.[35] Christ was the visible God and therefore "other" from the immutable and transcendent Father. By the mid-fourth century such a perspective is considered the worst of heresies by later fourth century writers. Hilary exemplifies this when he writes:

> There is the opinion of some that on account of his condition, sorrow had occurred in God and the fear of his coming passion weakened him because he said, *My soul is sorrowful unto death*

---

34. *On Christian Suffering* 12.13.

35. See Justin *Dialogue with Trypho*: "... it is written that sweat poured out like drops when he prayed, *If possible, let this cup pass.* Clearly his heart was trembling and his bones likewise—his heart seemed like wax melting inside of him. This is so that we would know that the Father wished his own son to be genuinely subject to such suffering ... (103.7–8).

(Matt 26: 38) and that *Father, if it is possible, let this cup be removed from me* . . . For they want to attach the distress that comes from the weakness of the body to his Spirit, as if the taking of flesh in its feeble condition detracted from that power of his incorruptible substance and eternity . . .[36]

And yet, never does Hilary, nor any writer in the fourth century, bring a condemnation to bear for the lack of orthodox sentiment found in earlier theologies. Only Tertullian is singled out for having committed an "error" in later life,[37] though this does not prevent Hilary from utilizing Tertullian's contributions toward an orthodox interpretation of the Lord's Prayer (Matthew 6).

Were not the ancients aware of the conflicting differences within their own positions? If they were aware, how could they knowingly have represented their faith in harmonious fashion with their forbears? Can we say that there existed a doctrinal "blind spot" generally applicable to patristic literature, as some contemporary historians have suggested? The implication here—we are told—is to focus our attention primarily on the ancients' rhetorical style and political circumstances rather than on the doctrinal presentations—which is exactly what a large number of scholars do. If this implication is at all accurate, then hundreds of treatises, commentaries, catechisms, hymns, etc., were produced with the (in part) intention of covering up the realities of churches' inability to share in unifying principles of agreement. This is, obviously, ridiculous. And when we put things in this way, the position of those who reject the viability of any sort of doctrinal orthodoxy does not sound so balanced and objective as they purport to be.

Over the span of four hundred years, the church's tradition underwent transformation that included a different stress on already familiar points, or, a shift to a more precise wording, or, the implicit realization that previous teaching was deficient in addressing current problems. The "labor" by which this process unfolded is no less instructive than the results. If there is a lesson to be learned that sits on the surface of this period, it is that doctrinal matters were taken quite seriously and were seen as indispensible to the construction of Christian identity. For post-moderns, the very intensity of these struggles over theological matters is baffling. I cannot

---

36. Hilary *Commentary on Matthew* XXXI.2.

37. Ibid., V.1: "the subsequent error of the man has detracted from the authority of his commendable writings."

count how many times I have been asked why the early church fought so constantly and fiercely over doctrine, especially when the matter at stake seemed like a trifling one. Need we repeat Sherlock Holmes' rebuttal?—*there are no such things as trifles*. While we may not fully comprehend or appreciate the ancients' preoccupation with theological definition, we cannot dismiss it. One thing is for sure: we never hear of an ancient church intellectual apologize or express second thoughts about the worthiness of his or her cause for doctrinal exactitude. This is not necessarily a beneficial thing. It does, however, indicate that if we are eager to draw on the rich resources of the early church, we might start with the *anatomical study of their theological struggles*. By this I mean discovering and reflecting on the early church's writings more for their own sakes—as it were—than for our purposes of application. It is largely for this reason that I never allow a PhD student in patristics to write a dissertation that seeks to apply the ancients to some contemporary issue or problem. The time will come for that—I often explain—but it is not now. It is more important for students and scholars to enter the thought-world of the ancient churches and become acquainted with their own expressions and conceptions.

Let me return to T. S. Eliot as I bring this paper to a close. In his *Notes toward a Definition of Culture*, he contends that bringing about culture, including a Christian one, is not something you "can deliberately aim at." It is rather the result of the practice of a variety of more or less harmonious activities. For this reason, he says, "an ecclesiastical unity cannot be imposed in the hope that it will bring about a unity of faith, and a religious diversity cultivated for its own sake would be absurd."[38] Christian churches will never be able to establish a Christian culture grounded on worship and practices alone, nor will it occur by focusing on moral problems. The nurturing of a uniquely Christian identity necessarily raises pertinent questions about authority. In part, this will involve making decisions of determining what constitutes doctrine that is within the spirit of the ancient tradition and what is not. Without this determination, the hope for making a Christian culture will never be sustained.

---

38. T. S. Eliot, *Notes towards the Definition of Culture* in *Christianity and Culture* (New York: Harcourt, 1976) 92.

TWO

Authentic Participation in the Great Tradition

Tony Clark

In consideration of our topic, let me pose the following question: What does it mean to inhabit the "Great Tradition" of Anglicanism *authentically*? To begin, it is important to acknowledge that the nature and development of the Great Tradition, and the broader tradition of the Christian church of which it is a part, has been conceived in a variety of ways. A recent and highly distinctive perspective is offered in Phyllis Tickle's book, *The Great Emergence: How Christianity is Changing and Why*. Published in 2008, it has reached a wide readership. The book deals with the way in which Christianity has emerged over time, with a particular emphasis upon the contemporary situation. Its purview is not limited to the Anglican tradition, although its author is a lay Eucharistic minister of the Episcopal Church in the United States of America. In the light of the book's popularity, and the proximity of its subject matter to the theme of this conference, it seems timely to consider its claims.

The Great Emergence

The basic thesis of the book is that the church in the Western world and beyond is going through an upheaval of monumental proportions as part of a broader transforming movement that is reconfiguring our culture. This process *is* the "Great Emergence," and we find ourselves caught up in the middle of it.

This phenomenon of radical transformation, in which the church and society must re-establish their identities and authority structures, is something that happens every five hundred years, according to Tickle. As she puts it, every five hundred years the church has a "huge rummage sale." We are now in the midst of the Great Emergence, which is the most recent and, in Tickle's estimation, the most radical of such rummage sales. The previous events and processes she identifies are the "Great" Reformation (1517 CE); the Great Schism (1051 CE); the Council of Chalcedon (451 CE), along with the decline of the Roman Empire in the fifth century and the life of Gregory the Great (540–604 CE). Before that was The Great Transformation—which is the term she gives to the period in which Christianity was born (70 CE).[1]

Every five hundred years the church is propelled into one of these periods of tumult and transformation, and there is not a whole lot we can do about it. Tickle writes, "When Christians despair of the upheavals and re-formulations that have been the history of our faith—when the faithful resist, as so many do just now, the presence of another time of reconfiguration with its inevitable pain—we all would do well to remember that, not only are we in the hinge of a five-hundred-year period, but we are the direct product of one."[2] The thought that we are caught up in a process over which we have no influence is expressed again towards the end of the book when Tickle asks, "Where is this thing going, even as it is carrying all of us along with it in its mad career?"[3]

In addition to propounding this dialectical schema, in which both church and society are caught up, the book describes some of the particular changes that have been brought about through these periods of "storm and stress." In the Great Reformation, for example, *sola scriptura*—

---

1. See Tickle, *The Great Emergence: How Christianity Is Changing and Why* (Grand Rapids: Baker, 2008) 19–31.
2. Ibid., 26–27.
3. Ibid., 116.

scripture alone—was established as the principle of authority in what was the emergent church at that time.[4] One of the characteristics of the current upheaval is, according to Tickle, the demise of *sola scriptura* as a locus of authority, and the emergence of the Holy Spirit in its place.[5] Another feature of the emerging or emergent church is the rejection of Christian particularity and exclusivity. Such, it is claimed, are the discernable contours of the new church arising out of the Great Emergence. The book has much more to say, and offers some thoughtful insights. Nevertheless, it exhibits some serious deficiencies. I will consider a few of them.

First, I am skeptical about one of the basic premises of the book, which is that the church, and society at large, goes through a period of radical transformation every five hundred years. This is a crude characterization that serves as much to confuse as to clarify. What, for example, are we are supposed to make of the Enlightenment, which bisects the Great Reformation and the Great Emergence? How is the Renaissance to be located in the scheme?

There is also a strange Hegelian tinge to Tickle's description of the cycles of upheaval, transformation, and consolidation. The suggestion is that we are "carried along" by these processes that bring us to new and higher levels of consciousness. It is interesting that the Reformation's emphasis upon the authority of Scripture, or *sola scriptura*, yields to the authority of the Holy Spirit in the believer's life in the Great Emergence. The reason offered for this is that since the Reformation there have been a variety of issues in which the authority of the Bible's teaching has been called into question. In matters such as slavery, divorce, and the ordination of women, among others, the church has established the way forward, in Tickle's view, in opposition to the *sola scriptura* principle. She asserts that the final issue, which will settle the matter once and for all, is the gay issue. She writes, "When it [the gay issue] is all resolved—and it most surely will be—the Reformation's understanding of Scripture as it had been taught by Protestantism for almost five centuries will be dead . . .

---

4. This was a slogan of the Protestant Reformation whereby it sought to locate the church's authority in Holy Scripture rather than ecclesial tradition and papal pronouncement. See Tickle, *Great Emergence*, 45–46.

5. Over against the implication in Tickle's comment, it should be noted that the Reformers would scarcely have regarded the *sola scriptura* principle and the Holy Spirit of God as alternative sources of authority!

Of all the fights, the gay one must be—has to be—the bitterest, because once it is lost, there are no more fights to be had. It is finished."[6]

If Tickle's broad theory is correct, the outcome of the current debate about human sexuality was decided before it began. The real significance of the debate is that its conclusion will signal the death knell for the *sola scriptura* principle. This being the case, the current discussion of the gay issue is entirely spurious, because the new paradigm of the Great Emergence will inevitably sweep away the very scriptural basis upon which many orthodox Christians are seeking to address the matter.[7] In sum, the book claims to have identified the pattern of history's ineluctable march to enlightenment, at least in as far as this is manifest in the church.

It is not difficult to see the attraction of the book's thesis to a wide audience as it touches on two ideas to which many are drawn. We like to think that we possess the key that unlocks the secrets of history—and, perhaps, even the mind and purposes of God. Moreover, we are fond of imagining that we live in historic times; that the particular moment in which we live is charged with significance. The book offers generous helpings of both ideas and, I would submit, this is why its proposals are attracting attention.

Returning to the Question

Returning to the question posed at the outset, "What does it mean to inhabit the "Great Tradition" of Anglicans *authentically*? *The Great Emergence* was

---

6. Tickle, *Great Emergence*, 101.

7. An excellent example of a study that attempts to address the theme of homosexuality from a broadly Reformed perspective is Oliver O'Donovan's *Church in Crisis: The Gay Controversy and the Anglican Communion* (Eugene, OR: Cascade, 2008). This is a thoughtful and nuanced study that acknowledges that the gay controversy, as a relatively new controversy, raises critical questions for the Reformed tradition. O'Donovan criticizes both conservative approaches that are prone to using biblical texts to bolster pre-established negative attitudes to gay relationships, and liberal approaches that presuppose the authenticity of gay relationships and sweep aside any aspect of the biblical tradition that might call that authenticity into question. While for Tickle the gay issue sounds the death knell for the Reformed tradition (or the *sola scriptura* principle), for O'Donovan the controversy calls those of the Reformed tradition to a period of reflection through which they seek to discern more of what is implied in their tradition about the issue of human sexuality.

not written to answer this question and, obviously, there was no obligation for it to do so. Nevertheless, there is something disturbing about some of the knowledge-claims made in the book. Let me explain.

The book contends that it has identified the dynamic process—one might call it "the grand historical scheme"—by which the church emerges through successive periods of struggle. But from whence comes the knowledge of this grand scheme by which church's history is to be interpreted and evaluated? No explicit answer to this question is offered. The author simply presumes that she occupies a perspective from which all the events and struggles her book portrays can be surveyed. It is not from an *attachment* to any particular epoch of the church's evolution, but from a perspective *detached* from them all—even the period of the Great Emergence into which we have now supposedly entered. One might say it presumes to offer, to borrow a phrase from Thomas Nagel, a "view from nowhere."

But the idea of a detached, "tradition-less" perspective, with its pretentions to value-free objectivity, has been subjected to fierce critiques in recent years. Alasdair MacIntyre's *Whose Justice? Which Rationality?* is just one contribution—although a particularly articulate and influential one—to a substantial movement that calls into question such modernist, objectivist pretentions.[8] One of the emphatic assertions of this movement is that all knowledge is perspectival. Or, to put it another way, we cannot have a view of things apart from the tradition, or traditions, we inhabit. The view from nowhere is a view that is simply not available to us.

We might think of an analogy here.[9] To communicate effectively with one another we must use a particular language. We must know this language at least well enough to be able to focus on the meaning we wish to convey rather than the grammar and vocabulary we will, inevitably, use to express it. The language we use is not an absolute expression of our meaning. Although we can enrich our use of language in various ways, there is always a sense in which any language places constraints on our communication. And yet the very language that limits our communication is utterly indispensible if we are to say anything at all. To cease to use

---

8. Alasdair MacIntyre, *Whose Justice? Which Rationality* (Notre Dame: University of Notre Dame Press, 1988).

9. Much of the following analysis draws on the thought of the scientist-philosopher Michael Polanyi. See, in particular, Polanyi, *Personal Knowledge: Towards a Post-Critical Philosophy* (London: Routledge, 1958). Cf. 59.

this language would be to cease communication, unless we learn a new language. And another language could only provide an additional "linguistic perspective," not a "linguistic absolute." If our use of language may be regarded as an analogy for our participation in a tradition, it becomes clear that we will unavoidably view the world from the perspective of the tradition in which we stand or, to use a word I prefer, we "indwell."[10]

This view of tradition does not commit us to relativism, though some have seen things in this way. However, it certainly does suggest that any interpretation of the history of the church that fails to recognize its own rootedness in a tradition necessarily lacks an essential self-awareness. One of the striking aspects of Tickle's account is its apparent detachment from any part in the developments it portrays. The proposed grand historical process by which the church emerges over the centuries is a concept that arises not from a perspective engendered by committed participation within a particular tradition; it presumes to be the "view from nowhere." It is curious, if not ironic, that an author so enamored with postmodernist narratives as is Phyllis Tickle should utilize a method that appears to be deeply indebted to a modernist outlook in general, and to a form of Hegelian idealism in particular.

If it is the case that we *necessarily* understand things from within a tradition, and that our various ways of knowing arise out of our participation within that tradition, it follows that this insight needs to be taken into account in interpreting the tradition and the ways in which it has evolved.

The View from Somewhere

If the idea of "the view from nowhere" is a deceptive myth, it is evident that we ought more properly to think in terms of "a view from somewhere." As I have said, the "somewhere" is the tradition (or traditions) in which we participate and to which we give our allegiance. I am, of course, thinking of the Christian tradition and this can be appropriately narrowed to the particular Christian tradition to which we are committed and which we "indwell."

Let me say a little about the nature of this "indwelling." I have suggested that knowledge of our own tradition, along with an understanding

---

10. "Indwelling" is a term extensively utilized by Michael Polanyi.

of its development, is necessarily perspectival and facilitated by our committed participation within it. But what does participation within that tradition look like? What constitutes it?

We are accustomed to describing Christian traditions or denominations in terms of theological statements or propositions. Here we will obviously think of the ancient creeds, confessions, and the kinds of doctrinal statements that are issued by the leadership of a given denomination from time to time. It is not surprising, therefore, that we tend to compare and contrast denominations on the basis of the particular articulate statements to which they claim to adhere. Indeed, it is typically on the basis of such statements that one group of Christians will determine if, and to what degree, they are willing to associate and co-operate with others. While I do not wish to deny the importance of creeds, confessions, and doctrinal statements, I want to challenge the commonly held belief that such articulate statements characterize what it means to inhabit the ecclesial traditions that espouse them.

There are at least two reasons why this might be so. First, there may be committed members of a Christian denomination who have reservations—and perhaps substantial reservations—about elements of the church's confessions. For example, how many contemporary Anglicans would be able to affirm, without reserve, all thirty-nine Articles of the 1662 Book of Common Prayer?[11] This is one sense in which the theological statements of the church might not adequately characterize what it means to indwell that denomination's tradition, although I do not want to pursue the point here.

A further reason for distinguishing between the articulate theological expressions of a church and the experience of indwelling its tradition may be regarded as obvious, and yet it is often overlooked. Our commitment to any tradition is manifest in our participation in the practices that constitute it. So, for example, what it means to indwell or inhabit the Anglican tradition is participation in the common liturgical forms of the church: the saying or chanting of psalms, listening to the public reading of Scripture, the singing of hymns, the praying of many different types of prayers (collects, confessions, intercessions, etc.), the celebration of the Eucharist, and all this in the very particular liturgical space of the church building that both facilitates and shapes these activities as corporate,

---

11. For example, not all would agree with article XVII, on the theme of predestination and election, as it is expressed in the 1662 Book of Common Prayer.

congregational practices. A great deal more could be said about public worship, and, beyond that, one could explore many other dimensions of the church's life: its ecclesial structures, its various pastoral ministries, its role in education, its care for the poor, its civic responsibilities, its prophetic witness to the wider society, etc.

To participate in the Anglican tradition—and there are, of course, direct parallels in other ecclesial traditions—is to engage in these kinds of things; to seek God and to serve God in and through them, and to be shaped as human beings in communion with God and with others, by participating in them.

Two Ways of Knowing

What we "know" through our involvement in regular corporate worship, or through our engagement in other aspects of the church's ministry, simply cannot be reduced to statements and propositions. It is, of course, possible to describe those things in which we are involved, at least to some degree. We can offer a description of Sunday worship, for example, but that is not to distill the essence of what it is to come before God in an act of corporate worship. The kind of knowledge contained within a description of worship is quite distinct from the kind of knowledge that attaches to our participation in it. We are dealing with two forms of knowing and, while they are evidently related, the nature of the relationship between one and the other may not be as clear and unproblematic as we might be inclined to think.

Let me illustrate the point with an example somewhat remote from the concerns of church and theology. Think of cycling. If you claim that you "know" how to ride a bicycle you are probably claiming that you could, at a moment's notice, hop on a bike and ride off without fear of failing or falling. But do you know the formula for balancing on a bicycle? Perhaps you don't because it is, as it turns out, a fiendishly complicated one. But, if you don't know this formula, how seriously can I take your claim to "know" how to ride a bicycle? After all, you don't even "know" how to balance on the thing! If we put things in this way it is clear enough that we are talking about two different (although related) kinds of knowledge. The first type of knowledge is manifest, in this case, in the form of an embodied skill: you can ride your bicycle. And, of course, you can ride your bicycle whether or not you know the formula for balancing. You can even ride your bicycle if you *think* you know the formula but, in fact, possess a mistaken formula! In these circumstances one might be tempted to say, "The formula is quite beside the point; what matters is whether one can cycle or not." This may be satisfactory up to a point, but it is a perfectly legitimate thing to try to *explain* a phenomenon, such as a person's ability to ride a bicycle. Is it not the case that a good explanation—a sound theory—is "knowledge"? Indeed, more generally, isn't the desire to explain an indispensible part of science and scientific discovery?

It is obvious that these two types of knowledge can and need to be distinguished. But we also need to be mindful that descriptive or articulate knowledge (the formula for balancing on a bicycle in this case) arises because there are people who have cycling skills (physicists do not typically devote their time to explaining phenomena that don't exist!). It is important to make this last point, because we are often inclined to think that it is our articulate knowledge—our explanations, formulae, statements, propositions, etc.—that are the *primary* truth-bearers. Or, to put it in another way, we habitually regard a good theory as the *basis* of good practice. What I want to say is that good theory often arises because there is good practice—or at least some level of practical know-how—which may become the theme of reflective theoretical endeavor. This is so because our articulate, or theoretical knowledge, is typically sourced by embodied or practical forms of knowledge.

Riding bicycles and living out one's faith in the context of the church are, I will acknowledge, very different sorts of phenomena. However, the parallels are not insignificant. If we are to talk about "the knowledge of faith" we must be aware of the relationship between articulate forms of faith—expressed in creeds, confessions, doctrinal statements, etc.—and the kinds of knowledge that arise through participation in the many and varied practices that comprise the life of the church.

I want to make one further substantial point about the relationship between the two types of knowledge. It relates to what I have already said through the example of cycling, but it identifies a very particular, important, and largely ignored aspect of the dynamic relationship between the two distinct forms of knowledge. In order to do this I want to approach again the example of language, although from a slightly different angle.

In using a familiar language we do not typically pay a great deal of conscious attention to its grammar and vocabulary. Rather, we are concerned with the meaning we intend to convey in the use of it. Our familiarity with the language instills within us the confident expectation that, as we seek to express ourselves, the words that we need will simply come to mind. We can do this because we "indwell" the language we are using. We might say we have "mastered it," or that we have "internalized it." The point is that we don't think *about* the language; we think *with* it. Indeed, to start thinking about vocabulary and grammar in the midst of the process of speaking or writing is likely to be debilitating and to actually inhibit communication. If we start thinking about vocabulary and grammar our mind is distracted from a proper focus on the meaning, which is our primary concern.

This is not to deny that studying grammar provides us with a means of reflecting upon the way in which we ordinarily use language and can help us gain precision and avoid error. Working on vocabulary may enhance the effectiveness of our language usage. But there is a curious sense in which studying grammar represents a kind of "time-out" from our ordinary uses of language. Through such study we seek to add breadth and attain greater accuracy in the forms of speech that we adopt. But this goal is only achieved when we can appropriate the lessons we have learned without needing to think about them. As I have said, the ordinary way of using language is not to think *about* it, but to think *with* it.

We are all very effective language-users long before we become aware of grammar as a discipline. No four-year-old child has studied grammar in this way and so, in one sense of the word, we might say that such a child knows nothing of grammar. However articulate she or he may be, the child does not know the grammatical apparatus by which language is analyzed and represented, but the child *does* know grammar—and a great deal of it—because she or he has learned to participate in the linguistic practices of those by whom she or he has been nurtured. The child comes to indwell "language practices"—typically those of the parental household. At four years a child's language skills will not be fully developed but they will be very advanced, despite the absence of any formal grammatical knowledge.

Indwelling the Great Tradition

It is my hope that this discussion of language and grammar will be helpful in illuminating the points I now want to make about the Great Tradition of Anglicanism in this final section.

What does it mean to participate in, or to indwell, the Great Tradition? I want to say that, *primarily*, it means that one places oneself in the midst of those practices that constitute the tradition. It means that one participates in corporate worship; that one engages in prayers of adoration, confession, and intercession, etc.; that one says the psalms and sings hymns and songs to the praise of God in the congregation of worshippers; that one grows in awareness of the narrative of the Christian story through the ministry of the Word—and especially the public reading of Scripture and preaching—as it arises out of the richly textured liturgical year; that one is baptized and shares in the bread and wine of the Eucharist; that one seeks to care for one's neighbors and to share the Good News of Gospel; and that one opens oneself to the transforming work of the Holy Spirit in and through such things.

What we "know" through our participation in all of these practices is not something that can be reduced to descriptions, nor can the meaning of what we know be captured in doctrinal statements. In saying this I emphasize again that I do not wish to disparage creedal and doctrinal statements, or suggest that we dispense with them. To the contrary, I affirm that they must have an honored place within the tradition, guiding the faithful and guarding them against error. The church has typically come to such statements and affirmations after careful theological thought, prayerful reflection, and maybe a good deal of heated debate (and perhaps even a little beard tugging!). Nevertheless, these articulate expressions of faith can be no more than highly abbreviated summaries of the deep knowledge established through participation in the practices which constitute the tradition. The issue is not that the creeds and confessions are irrelevant or misleading, but that they cannot convey the kind of knowledge which arises through a full-orbed participation within the tradition. Creeds and confession cannot function as a substitute for committed participation in the practices that constitute the Great Tradition—or any other tradition of the church. Nor could they have arisen apart from the kind of knowledge established through such participation.

Of course, none of this should surprise us if we have paid attention to the Gospel accounts of how Jesus called and nurtured his first disciples. Jesus' apprenticing of the Twelve was not devoid of elements of didactic teaching, but the fundamental command of Jesus to each of his disciples was: "Follow me." Or, if I might be permitted to expand, "Come along with me, see what I'm doing, and learn what it means to have a part in it."

Conclusion

At the outset I posed the question, "What does it mean to inhabit the "Great Tradition" of Anglicanism *authentically*?" To the accusation that I have scarcely started to answer this question I can only reply that I am guilty as charged. Nevertheless, what I hope to have done is to show that if we are going to interpret the Great Tradition authentically we must do so from the perspective afforded to us *through* a deep, committed indwelling of the practices that constitute that tradition. While it is important to acknowledge the significance of creedal and confessional formulations, we must be mindful of the very general truth that our knowledge of the tradition will always transcend what we are able to articulate of it. We know more than we can tell.

I hope that I have also demonstrated something of the problematic nature of a project such as the one undertaken by Phyllis Tickle in her book, *The Great Emergence*. The claim that the Christian tradition is radically reconstituted every five hundred years is questionable in a number of ways, a few of which I have noted. In closing I would like to ask a couple of questions that might provide the basis for further discussion of the book's claims. Firstly, if Tickle is correct in her assertion that we are being carried along by dynamic forces that are beyond our influence, we must ask whether it is meaningful to talk about "inhabiting the tradition authentically," at least in a transitional moment such as we find ourselves in at the moment? One can scarcely "inhabit" a tradition characterized by such fundamental discontinuity.

The second question is closely related to the first: if the periods of turmoil and transformation are as radical as Tickle suggests, might it be more appropriate to think of such developments in Christianity in terms of *successive* stages within traditions, given that the emergent tradition is always substantially incommensurate with the tradition out of which it has arisen?[12] If this is so, the kind of analysis I have offered is evidently redundant. But I think this is the point at which Tickle has strayed furthest from the heart of Christianity. Tickle characterizes the Great Emergence as the dissolution of exclusive Christian claims along with

---

12. The influence of Thomas Kuhn's ideas of scientific revolutions may be at work, consciously or unconsciously, in this aspect of Tickle's thinking. See Kuhn, "The Structure of Scientific Revolutions," in the *International Encyclopedia of Unified Science*, eds. Otto Neurath, Rudolf Carnap, and Charles Morris, Vol. 2, No. 2 (Chicago: University of Chicago Press, 1970).

the Reformation's *sola scriptura* principle. I would answer that two of the *abiding* characteristics of the Christian tradition are, firstly, its insistence upon the uniqueness of Christ and, secondly, its conviction that it must always return to Holy Scripture as its primary authority in its witness to God's revelatory self-disclosure in Christ. What we do *not* have in the Christian tradition is the emergence, through some dialectical process, of an all-encompassing, undifferentiated religious consciousness.[13]

It is my conviction that the Christian tradition is characterized by a far greater degree of continuity than Tickle allows. The church is dynamic: its practices, and the theological convictions it endeavors to articulate, are not static.[14] The church must continue to listen to the call and command of God by the faithful indwelling of the traditions that it has inherited. As participants in the Great Tradition of Anglicanism we may rest assured that there will always be room within it for growth and diversity, just as there will always be a need for reform. As a dynamic tradition its well-being will be best served by a healthy capacity for self-critique and a disciplined, faithful imagination. We will never exhaust the possibilities embedded within this tradition if, as participants within it, we place our trust in the God who called it into being. In this way the Great Tradition of Anglicanism will be preserved even as it is constantly called to renewal in the power of the Holy Spirit.

---

13. I take it that this would be a fair characterization of Tickle's position.

14. Due to limitations of space, I have been unable to pursue the question of authentic transformation or evolution.

THREE

Presumption, Preparation, *Parrēsia*, *Perichōrēsis*, and Worship

Edith Humphrey

Whatever one thinks of the animism and ideals of the Disney movie *The Lion King*, the weighty effect of the opening scene is undeniable. The music, with its chant undecipherable except to the few who know Zulu, nevertheless communicates its message of anticipation and welcome:

> *Nants ingonyama bagithi Baba* (Here comes a lion, Father)
> *Sithi uhm ingonyama* (Oh yes, it's a lion)
> *Siyo Nqoba* (We're going to conquer)

The music swells, coming to a climax as the priestly primate presents the newborn prince to the host of animals far below. "Oh yes, it's a lion; we're going to conquer!" The lion-cub looks down, wide-eyed, as animals of every kind stamp for joy. A ray of glory from the unveiling cloud-cover is trained upon the young messiah, and the whole assembly bows the knee and closes their eyes in reverence. The first time I saw this, its joyous sobriety brought tears to my eyes, despite the accompanying trite lyrics about the "circle of life." The juxtaposition between old and young, awkward and beautiful, opened and closed eyes, near and far, is evocative of life with all its complexity and simplicity. And the whole extravaganza, the spectacle of it all, is an apt preparation for the epic leonine drama to follow: even the unwilling are ushered into the story. We have been wooed by wonder.

The Problem of Wonder

The experience of being overwhelmed, of being overcome, by astonishment is basic to the human condition. As another song in *The Lion King* puts it, when we are faced with some luminous experiences, "It's enough for this wide-eyed wanderer/That we got this far . . . It's enough to make kings and vagabonds/Believe the very best."

In my own life, three such vignettes stand out.

In the first, I am in the back of my parents' car, a five-year-old who has just become the incredulous owner of a golden cocker spaniel puppy. It is almost Christmas, and the snow is swirling around the car as we return home from the farm. I sit in the back, a newspaper between my coat and the squirming puppy, with tears streaming down my face. "What's the matter?" asked my mom, "Don't you like her?" I can hardly choke out the words, "I can't believe she's here!" For me, Advent is over, and the New Jerusalem has descended—and the lump in my throat matches the fullness of my heart.

Second scene: Again, I am with my parents. It is very early on Easter Sunday and we aren't in our usual place, the red brick Salvation Army Corps where I would worship for twenty years, and from which I would be married. Normally at Easter I would have been wakened early by my folks to go and stir enormous pots of scrambled eggs in the kitchen for the crowd that would come down after the sunrise service. Instead, we have finally found a parking space for the car in downtown Washington, DC, trekked a long way up a hill to an enormous stone church, and are watching a man in a strange hat banging on the huge wooden door with a staff. As we go through the doors, to the strains of the organ, I hear my dad say, "There's no seating. Shall we forget it?" "No," says my mom, "let's stay until she [referring to me] gets restless." Restless? The singing is glorious, the smell intoxicating, the whole thing wonderful and most wonderful. We stayed for the whole Easter service, standing through my first experience of a traditional liturgy.

The final picture is much later than the first two, and of a different sort. I am beyond exhaustion, physical and emotional. I have slept at the hospital for four nights, on the little cot beside my father, who knows that I am there, but who hasn't been able to speak for some time. For awhile we had hoped that he would pull out of the downward spiral, but this morning I know better. His breathing has changed now, that strange stop-and-start breathing that spells out the end. Others are gathering, trying to be kind, but it is almost as though my mom, my dad and I are alone in the room. Once or twice I think it is over, and then, it becomes apparent that it really almost is. Something is gradually changing in my father's entire appearance, and then, there it is; or rather, there it isn't. My dad hasn't been himself for years, but this is entirely different. In the place of a vibrant, though ill person, there is his beloved body, but I don't see his eyes smiling out any more. The peace is a relief, after all his effort. But there is something else happening to me besides that commingling of relief and grief. I am amazed: how is it possible that this strange yet still familiar body *lived*, that it ever spoke, laughed, argued, walked on the beach, read books with me? Somehow, by watching life ebb away, I have been reminded of the wonder of creation—God molded the man, and breathed life into him, and he became a living being! At the threshold of death, I am compelled to remember the Creator. My cousin, who is the official minister at the death-watch, asks if I want to pray. I do, and, oddly, it is a prayer of thanksgiving.

Joy, wonder, fear, and awe. When I was four, five, and nearly fifty. Through one of his tiny creatures, through ceremony, and through death, God had forcibly borne down upon my life, taking me out of myself, reminding me of the tenderness, the hugeness, the strangeness of what we experience every day. Everywhere there are new puppies, everywhere people send up hymns to the Lord, every minute someone's beloved father dies. Yet these commonplace things served as windows to a world of wonder, a world that is made to praise God.

The experience of being overwhelmed is basic to the human condition. Perhaps it is only natural that a young child should be mesmerized by worship. But why is it not *always* natural for us? Where has the wonder gone? What is it about our worship that makes us blasé? Perhaps we should ask, what is it about *us*? Is familiarity the problem? I do not think that it is simply that familiarity breeds contempt. Because, you know, it needn't. Think of the toddler who wants that same story again and again, or the adolescent who wants to hear her favorite song one more time, or my husband who listens repeatedly in the car to scratched recordings of the Goon Show (now digitized) until I think I will go *mad*. No, it isn't our familiarity that takes away wonder; it is something else.

Could it be that we are fearful of too luminous a meeting with God? Consider the adolescent who has misbehaved and knows that his father is going to "have a talk" with him. Several strategies might be adopted by the delinquent kid—avoidance, rebellion, deceit. Or, there is the more sophisticated strategy of nonchalance: "Um, yes, I did smoke that cigarette that you left on the coffee-table, but you know, it is important for me to have new experiences, and I didn't really like it, anyway. I tell you what, Dad, you stop smoking, and I'll promise never to take another one of your cigarettes? Deal?" And so it is that even Christians frequently have approached God with deliberate casualness—down-playing the meeting, talking to God in the business-like language of contract and exchange. Casual worship can be a pre-emptive move to mitigate our fear. Certainly I myself have kept God at arm's length by doing my duty in worship or in personal devotions, adding it onto a long list of other things that I must accomplish: no wonder that, unprepared for God's mystery and unrepentantly distracted by other concerns, the worship is flat. I have avoided staying quiet long enough in my personal prayer times to allow the full weight of God's presence to impose. Who knows what I might be shown about myself, or what other reality might disturb my cherished presuppositions?

Then there is a reaction, in contrast to the dutiful mode. Do we think that creating the worship moment is *our* job? Worried that, for many people, worship lacks life, worship leaders strive to make the moment meaningful, to amplify its significance by adding a touch of color, a dash of emotion, a new symbol, a rush of engineered excitement. Such a move is common in various evangelical traditions. Here there are those who think that it is their role to be what sociologists call "psychopomps"—leaders of the soul who initiate worshippers into the mystical world. A complementary action follows among the worshippers themselves, who learn all kinds of ways to excite their own emotions, and mistake this passion for an authentic meeting with God.

These approaches to worship are born of faithlessness. The first casual or contractual approach comes from fear that God does not know how to velvet his claws, so to speak. The second meddling approach comes from fear that God may not appear at all, that we are the only actors in the service or the meeting. At these extremes, corporate worship is rendered a hum-drum business affair, or an orgy of hysteria and melodrama. The depressive pole is seen in the group known as Jehovah's Witness. Have you ever attended their services? *So* serious. *So* dutiful. *So* devoid of joy or wonder. The manic pole is present in other cult meetings, such as those surrounding Vernon Howell, whose rhetoric so swept away his followers that they truly believed themselves to be part of the cosmic drama led by their very own Lamb, David *Koresh*, whose adopted "surname" is really a Persian rendering of the term "the Christ." But these problems are not limited to the cults. We see them in mainstream churches as well. Our dilemma concerning worship is a complex one in the West, for many of us retain the Protestant reaction to the "magical view" of the sacraments that we believe was inculcated in the Middle Ages. And yet we yearn for awe.

What is to be done to regain the mode of anticipation and welcome that matches our Servant King, our majestic and tender God? One of the prescriptions enjoined both in the Scriptures and in the traditional liturgies of East and West is that we come to worship, and enter gradually into worship, by the gate of *preparation*. If appropriate means of preparation for the great meeting with God are in place, we will not easily don the attitude of casual indifference. Indeed, if we use God's own means of preparation, then we will be given eyes to see and ears to hear the wonders that are truly there. We will not be tempted to engineer worship or to monitor our responses, priming the pump of the "meaningful." ("Come on, sing this wonderful song with joy!" urges the song-leader; Or the pastor instructs: "Listen to the wonderful words of this anthem, and let them move your heart.")

In the following pages, I will be talking about four "P"s and their relationship to worship—presumption, preparation, *parrēsia* and *perichōrēsis*. Though I will engage in some critique of attitudes and worship practices that are common to many churches of the West, be assured that what I am sharing with you is part of a steep learning curve for me, not something that I have attained! So let me begin with presumption.

Presumption

Here, again, I go back in my memory—over twenty-five years ago! My husband and I are worshipping in a new venue, and find some of the elements of the service familiar, but others very odd. Salvationists in an evangelical Anglican service are not exactly fish out of water, but there are some clashing presuppositions. We come to the general confession. I examine the words intently:

> Most merciful God, we confess that we have sinned against you in thought, word, and deed, by what we have done, and by what we have left undone. We have not loved you with our whole heart; we have not loved our neighbor as ourselves. We are truly sorry and we humbly repent. For the sake of your Son Jesus Christ, have mercy on us and forgive us, that we might delight in your will and walk in your ways, to the glory of your name.[1]

Puzzled, I write on the side of the bulletin, communicating with my husband so as not to disturb those around us: "Don't these people believe that they are Christians? It sounds like they think they have to get saved all over again!" Then comes the absolution, and again I am concerned. Don't these friends know already that God forgives? Why do they need somebody to reassure them of it? And what right does that man have to talk in God's own voice, anyway?

The same kind of cognitive dissonance is often expressed by friends and family who come to my new-found church home, observing their first Eastern Orthodox church service: "Why do they keep saying over and over, 'Lord have mercy'? Don't they believe that He *has*?"

Of course, there are some serious theological issues here that we could discuss, and this would take days. Can I simply say that many who have come from backgrounds like mine have mistakenly believed that the dissonance comes from their theological convictions about justification, when frequently we are simply displaying garden-variety human "presumption"—presumption that we are a-okay, that it's all done, that we have "arrived," that God doesn't care about our sin, that it is unnecessary to persist in prayer, for, after all, God has already answered us.

Are corporate prayers for mercy and forgiveness vain repetition? Do repeated requests for God's mercy, or repeated repentance, signal a lack of faith in God's love? Consider what Jesus commends to his followers when he gives instruction in prayer. When the disciples asked Jesus to teach them to pray, what did he do? He gave them a template, a model, a set of words, phrases that together express humility and expectation

---

1. This contemporary form of the confession may be found on page 191 of *The Book of Alternative Services of the Anglican Church of Canada* (Toronto: Anglican Book Centre, 1985).

before God: "hallowed be thy name," "Give us this day," "forgive us," "Lead us not into temptation," "Deliver us from evil," "For thine is the glory." Doesn't God *know* that he is holy, and don't we? Why ask daily for our needs? Why ask that we be forgiven, if we already are? Why ask the Lord that he not test us? Do we expect that he would, if we don't ask to be excused? And do we expect that our loving Father would actually refuse to be our deliverer? And why finish by speaking about his glory? Surely he does not need us to pat him on the back! But this is the nature of the prayer that Jesus passes on to his followers. Surely this prayer is utterly realistic, matching our nature and our needs to the character and will of God Almighty.

Remember, too, that Jesus commended the Publican, who lowered his eyes, beat his breast and cried out "God, be merciful to me, a sinner!" (Luke 18:9-14).[2] There is no whiff of the idea that this kind of prayer is only suitable for the first-time penitent, for the would-be convert! Rather, Jesus tells the parable to the religious, to those who might presume upon the grace of God. And in Luke's Gospel the parable comes just after Jesus' comforting words concerning the repeated prayers of God's own people, "his elect, who cry to him day and night." To those who pray persistently, like the widow, Jesus says, God will grant justice! (Luke 18:7-8). Then there is the sobriety of Paul himself, the apostle of justification: "It is not as though I have already attained . . . but I strain towards the goal!" (Phil 3:12-14). And there is the strong warning in the book of Hebrews, that we should not presume, like the Hebrews in the wilderness, that we belong to God, but that we should, paradoxically, "*strive* to enter his *rest*" (Heb 3:7—4:13). Finally, there is the Word of God himself, calling in yearning to his people in John's Apocalypse, "Come out of her, my people" (Rev 18:4). God's call to action matches the description in another vision that his people have "washed their robes, and made them white" (Rev 7:14), so that at the end they will be as a bride, adorned for her husband (Rev 21:2).

We haven't time to work out the grave and substantive theological debates that have led to Protestant squeamishness concerning repeated calls for God's mercy, or even for the need of ongoing repentance. However, the passages above, including Jesus' own teaching on prayer, should put a brake on soteriological over-confidence. Here are three principles that may be helpful:

---

2. Citations from Scripture, except where marked, follow the RSV or my own translation from the original languages.

- A theology of justification should not lead us away from an earnest search for holiness.
- A theology of Jesus' victory should not lead us to be unreal about our continued sin.
- A theology of security in God's love should not lead to careless presumption.

Let's pause to consider these principles. When we rejoice in our acceptance by God, revel in Jesus' conquest of sin and death, and "rest" in the mercy of God, we must place these assurances within the context of all the Gospels and letters of the New Testament. After all, there are scriptural challenges to be held in tension with our joy and confidence: our acquittal by God in Christ does not neutralize the warnings regarding judgment that starts with the household of God (1 Pet 4:17); though Jesus has died for us, we are to take up the cross daily (Luke 9:23); though the Spirit gives confidence, we are to take heed that we do not fall (Heb 2:1). Protestant confidence in justification has, unfortunately, led to suspicion and avoidance of passages such as the book of James, or the words of Jesus concerning the importance of Torah in Matthew. This means that we may be in danger of not hearing "the whole counsel of God."

In short, we need to read the whole of Scripture—and, I would say, read the whole of Scripture in concert with the universal church. This means to sustain the paradox found throughout the New Testament, a paradox that has generally to do with the inter-relationship of grace and human activity, and specifically with our approach to worship: "work out your ... salvation in fear and trembling, for it is God at work in you" (Phil 2:12–13); "strive to enter that rest" (Heb 4:11). A reading of the book of Hebrews will put away any notion that the new covenant people may approach God with less awe than did the Israelites!

Preparation

So much for presumption. What is the alternative to such cheerful carelessness? It is to get and stay ready! There are several Hebrew words translated as "ready," associated with preparation for a meal (*'āśāh*), ritual readiness for war (*qādôš*), being stable or firm (*kûn*), and with "turning" or poising oneself (*pānāh*). The New Testament uses at least three Greek terms: *prothumos* (having to do with eagerness), *etoimos* (having to do with being equipped) and *paraskeuazō* (having to do with supplying what is necessary). From the beginning of the gospel, where the Baptist's task is to "make ready a people prepared for the LORD" (Luke 1:17–18),[3] through Jesus' parable that the bridesmaids be ready, and not presumptuous (Matt 25:10–11), through his warning to his disciples, "You also be ready: for the Son of Man will come unexpectedly" (Luke 12:40), through to his explanation to the sleeping disciples, "The spirit is truly ready, but the flesh is weak" (Mark 14:38), the theme of preparation sounds. Most luminous is that last night of Jesus' ministry: first, in John 13:10, Jesus speaks to Peter of the importance of washed feet (even for those who are largely already clean!); later, in John 15:3, he speaks of his disciples as branches who must be purged, or made clean by God's word.

How, then, are we made ready to worship? Of course, the radical preparation has been done in the God-Man, Jesus, who is not ashamed to call us brothers and sisters, and who has made us bold to pray "Our Father." We have been emboldened by the past work of God, but, as Jesus puts it, the Father is always working! This means that personally, corporately, and liturgically we need to be prepared to enter God's presence. In the Great Tradition of both East and West, the attentiveness required to enter God's presence is fostered by prayer and fasting. It may be that some have taken these resources mechanically, as if rote prayers and absence from food were a magic key, unlocking the gate to God's house. Since my childhood formation was in the non-sacramental Salvation Army, I understand well the arguments that familiarity breeds contempt and that human activities cannot in themselves unleash the Spirit, who is free. God can, of course, break through even when we are unprepared—yet at our best, we respond to the Spirit's work, and cry, "I will prepare him my heart."[4] Such inner preparation includes what our bodies are doing, for we are whole people.

Yet, we forget this, especially when our services are conceived in terms of theater or spectacle. A group of worshippers that jostles into the

---

3. I take the liberty here of referring to the Lord, using the Old Testament convention (though English translations do not do this in the New Testament), in order to indicate that the New Testament writer here is speaking specifically of YHWH, the "I AM" whom Moses also met, and who guided Israel.

4. The allusion is to Frank Gallio's Scripture song, "Exodus XV" (Stafford, TX: Mercy/Vineyard, 1982), but see also biblical wisdom about the prepared heart in Job 11:13. In 1 Chron 29:18 and Ps 10:17, it is God himself who prepares the human heart!

worship space, chatting and distracted, depends upon the worship leader to call their attention to the deep words of the hymn or Scripture song, to repeat again the words of the Scripture, in case they have not been heard, to say to them, "Do you not feel the presence of the Lord?" But these mediating actions themselves can be self-defeating. They highlight the mood, the mechanics, the vehicle of our praise, rather than pointing to the Lord. If we come with quiet hearts, determining to set aside competing thoughts, and to enter into worship from the beginning, then those leading us will not be tempted to act as stage directors. The words of the Preacher are salutary:

> Guard your steps when you go to the house of God. To draw near to listen is better than to offer the sacrifice of fools, for they do not know that they are doing evil. Be not rash with your mouth, nor let your heart be hasty to utter a word before God, for God is in heaven and you are on earth. Therefore let your words be few. (Eccl 5:1–2)

It is a tricky thing, of course, to talk about attitude. Let us get more concrete and consider the importance of simple penitence: repentance for our brashness, for our carelessness, for all those things that we have done both deliberately and unwittingly. Repentance, in the Scriptures, is not simply an entry requirement to the following of Jesus, but it is ongoing. Perhaps the clearest evidence of this is seen in the Gospel of John, where we hear of multiple "turnings" towards the Lord Jesus, and not simply a single crisis of conscience. Consider Mary Magdalene, Thomas, and Peter, and how on Easter morning they are *several* times led to "turn."[5] We need to be continually realigned, for the flesh—what we are as fallen human beings—is weak. This is not a matter of distrusting God: it is rather to allow a sober realism to accompany our Christian joy.

What does this mean, practically, in terms of worship? It means that we prepare, both personally and corporately, to come into God's presence. Historical liturgies actually work by means of preparation, leading worshippers up the stairs, and into God's presence. In less liturgical settings, singing has been used for this purpose, in the recognition that folks often rush to church, and need to settle in. John Wesley commented that the

---

5. For an analysis of Johannine passages on repentence, see Humphrey, "'And I Shall Heal Them'—Repentance, Turning and Penitence in the Johannine Writings," in *Repentance in Christian Theology*, eds. Mark Boda and Gordon T. Smith (Collegeville, MN: Liturgical, 2006) 105–26.

holy Eucharist can be a converting ordinance, but he would have been horrified had he been able to foresee that some Christian communities in our day would make this the rule! He was, after all, living in a day when Christianity was the norm, and when those who believed intellectually needed for their hearts to be warmed: he was not speaking about admitting unbaptized pagans directly to the table. "Conversion" in the sense that he meant it was when someone who was a cold Christian met the Lord in the Eucharist, and was taken to a deeper level. But his regard for the utter holiness of the Eucharist is clear from his writings, and from his brother Charles's hymns—though we have forgotten some of the hymns about the Supper![6]

> Endless scenes of wonder rise
> With that mysterious tree,
> Crucified before our eyes
> Where we our Maker see:
> Jesus, Lord, what hast Thou done?
> Publish we the death Divine,
> Stop, and gaze, and fall, and own
> Was never love like Thine!
>
> Who can say how bread and wine
> God into man conveys?
> *How* the bread His flesh imparts,
> *How* the wine transmits His blood,
> Fills His faithful people's hearts
> With all the life of God!
>
> Sure and real is the grace,
> The manner be unknown;
> Only meet us in Thy ways,
> And perfect us in one.
> Let us taste the heavenly powers;
> Lord, we ask for nothing more:
> Thine to bless, 'tis only ours
> To wonder and adore.

Today, in some places we have tables that are completely unhedged, on the precept that Jesus ate and drank with sinners. Now we have some churches using the Lord's Supper as a way of limbering up the congregation so that they will be better prepared to hear the Word, as though it is

---

6. F. Colquhoun, "Charles Wesley's Eucharistic Hymns," *Churchman* 63 (1949). Online: http://www.churchsociety.org/churchman/documents/Cman_063_2_Colquhoun.pdf.

the Scriptures that lead us to the holy place, and the Eucharist is merely an exercise in meditation.

Attention to why the historic church put the service of the Word before the Eucharist is needed! In the ancient church, both in the East and in the West, the Service of the Word was open to those who were inquiring, and to those who were preparing for baptism. The Eucharist, however, was kept separate because it was the height and depth of the people's corporate meeting with the Lord—as the Eastern divine liturgy puts it, "holy things are for the holy." (This pattern of asking the catechumens to leave prior to the Eucharist proper was so prevalent that the ancient Service of the Word was called "the Liturgy of the Catechumens" whereas the Eucharist was known as "the Liturgy of the Faithful.") As Jesus declared, the Word makes us clean (John 15:3). Then, cleansed by his Word, we enter into his life, receiving from him. We help each other in the service, as we come together before the Lord. There is both kneeling and standing, postures of penitence and boldness before our Father. The priest asks forgiveness of the people, instead of simply proclaiming pardon and absolution, because we are all leveled before the holiness of God. Standing before the gospel trains our bodies to receive the Lord, as our minds listen to the word and our spirits are enlivened. Proclaiming peace (and if need be, asking forgiveness) with each other is a requisite to the great event itself. As described by Alexander Schmemann,[7] the entire liturgy is one great action of entrance, and entrance, and even more entrance—like Reepicheep,[8] we are called "further up and further in." And as we leave behind our worries, we do not leave behind the world that we love, but carry it in our prayers before the throne of God.

The church year, itself, adds a further element of preparation, a rhythm of fasting and feasting for us, creatures who are in time. Prior to Easter, we "excommunicate" ourselves, so to speak—fasting from the Eucharist on Holy Friday, sitting in darkness, and even attentively standing outside the church building prior to the Easter liturgy. We do all this, in expectation that the light and the door and the meal can be opened to us by the Lord, and we can enter into his joy. It is not a matter of pulling

---

7. Schmemann, *The Eucharist* (Crestwood, NY: St. Vladimir's Seminary Press, 1987), 63.

8. Reepicheep is the brave mouse of C. S. Lewis' Narnian Chronicles. This character longs for true reality, and also invites others to join in this upward and inward movement throughout the final book of the series, *The Last Battle*. See especially the title of chapter 15.

long faces on Good Friday, or of "pretending" not to be redeemed prior to the Easter joy. Rather, we acknowledge that we are creatures of time, and that not all is yet healed—always there is more to die to sin, always more for the Lord to raise up. He has done it, and is doing it, and will do it! And so he charges us to prepare.

Presumption and preparation—where does holy boldness, called in the New Testament *parrēsia*, come in? And what is the difference between presumption and boldness?

Parrēsia

We are bold because God has, in Christ, made us his very own children. Children can be "at home" in God's house—though the salon is different from the rumpus room! *Parrēsia* is different from presumption, because it retains the quality of *wonder*. How wonderful that we should be called the children of God! St. Paul speaks about the ongoing wonder of the Christian in this way:

> Therefore, since we have been justified by faith, we have peace with God through our Lord Jesus Christ. Through him we have also obtained access by faith into this grace in which we stand, and we rejoice *in hope of the glory of God*. *More than that*, we rejoice in our sufferings, knowing that suffering produces endurance, and endurance produces character, and character produces hope, and hope does not put us to shame, because God's love has been poured into our hearts through the Holy Spirit who has been given to us. (Rom 5:1–5 ESV)

The Christian stance of hope is deliberate, looking to its foundations in the work of Jesus, and knowing that even suffering will bring fruit. We will not be ashamed, because our entire life is predicated on what God has done, is doing, and has promised to do. Even St. Paul, who persecuted Christians and so called himself "least of all" (1 Cor 15:9) possessed this character of holy boldness, and described it as having an "open face" before the Lord (2 Cor 3:16-18), as well as before his brothers and sisters (2 Cor 4:2; 2 Cor 6:11). We have boldness in knowing that we can actually bless the Lord, because he has enabled us to do this—isn't that a cheeky thought, that we could bless the Master of the universe? We have boldness to pray, boldness to worship—and we know that this is a marvel, that we are called to enter his presence and to participate in the priestly work of Jesus. This should not lead us to presumption, but increase our wonder.

Parrēsia, then, remembers that everything is a gift, that God is the initiator, but that he intends for us to walk on water, too. Godly boldness is characterized by gratitude, and moderated by remembering that we have not yet become all that we are meant to be. It holds on to the main thing, that God is our Father not by our nature, but because of the one who is the unique Son. He became poor that we might become rich.

Perichōrēsis

Let's finish, then, with a glance at the wonder of *perichōrēsis*, that mysterious relationship that there is between the Father, Son, and Holy Spirit. Full disclosure, here! I am on a crusade! It is urgent that we stop using arrogant words about our ability to understand and enter into the mystery of the Godhead. *Perichōrēsis* is the term used by the ancient theologians to speak about the mysterious interchange and unity of the Trinity. For example, speaking of the Father, Son and Holy Spirit, St. John Damascus explains: "The dwelling of the [divine] Persons is in each Other and is firmly established. For they are not separable, and do not part from each other, but they have their own proper *perichōrēsis* within one another, not so as to be dissolved together or commingled, but so as to cleave to each Other."[9] Contrary to the common wisdom, the term *perichōrēsis* does not come from the root noun *chōros* (meaning "chorus," as in Greek tragedy, or "dance") but from *chōra* (meaning "place"). *Perichōrēsis* therefore means "going around and beyond one's place" or "making room for." The word refers to the reciprocity, alternation, and interpenetration of the Persons of the Trinity. It was not meant to evoke anything so frivolous as a democratic round-dance, but is used to describe the great mystery by which Persons of the Holy Trinity occupy the same "space," yet are "near and towards" each other, in their distinctness. So the talk that we hear in some places about the "dance of the Trinity," and our entering blithely into that dance, is mistaken.

---

9. *Exposition of the Orthodox Faith* 1.14, my translation. For an online version, see http://www.ccel.org/ccel/schaff/npnf209.iii.iv.i.xiv.html.

It is urgent that we stop making the Holy Trinity into a mascot of our own human ideas, and allow God to be God. Looking at a passage from the well-known novel, *The Shack*, will show you why I am concerned:

> [Jesus is speaking] "That's the beauty you see in my relationship with Abba [the Father] and Sarayu [the Holy Spirit]. We are indeed submitted to one another and have always been so and always will be. Papa is as much submitted to me as I to him, or Sarayu to me, or Papa to her. Submission is not about authority and it is not obedience; it is all about relationships of love and respect. In fact, we are submitted to you [humans] in the same way."[10]

The theology of *The Shack* argues that obedience is not part of the relationship between Father, Son, and Holy Spirit, and not even a part of love. We hear otherwise in the Bible: "The Son only does what he sees the Father doing" (John 5:19); "The Son was made perfect in obedience" (Heb 5:8–9); "The [Holy] Spirit . . . shall glorify me" (John 16:13–14); "No one has seen the Father" (John 1:18; 6:46). There is an order in the Holy Trinity that does not rob the Persons of their mutuality, but expresses their love. The Spirit glorifies the Son who glorifies the Father. Yes, it is about love and respect: but it is also about authority and about obedience. These things are not mutually exclusive. Just as the Son is eternally begotten of the Father, and the Holy Spirit proceeds from all eternity from the Father, so the second and third Persons of the Trinity give glory to the Father, who is their eternal source: and yet they honor each other, each divine Person recognizing the other as God.

If the Son submits to the Father, let us have no loose talk about God submitting to us—though, ineffably, God did submit to the incarnation and crucifixion, and has so forged an astonishing way for us. Let us have no illusions about our entering the so-called dance of God as equal dancing partners. When we enter into that mysterious love of the Trinity, it is by means of our obedience, our honor, our giving glory to God! In Christ, we give our worthy praises to the Father; by the Spirit, we glimpse who God is, and enter into that light. How astonishing!

Jesus did not name God "our Father," without further clarification. Rather he said, "I am ascending to my Father and your Father" (John 20:17). It is by virtue of the one who is the unique Son that we are children of God; it is through the service of the high priest Jesus that we serve God

---

10 William P. Young, *The Shack* (Newbury Park, CA: Windblown, 2007) 145.

in worship; it is through the prophet Jesus that we speak the word of God truly; it is by the King of kings that we are made ruling priests to serve God. We are, even more than the Israelites before us, a royal priesthood whose major delight is to worship in wonder.

Given what we have seen concerning presumption, preparation, *parrēsia* and *perichōrēsis*, I'd like to suggest some specifics for those who are given to lead worship. Though these come from one who is used to a liturgical style in the context of "blended worship," they can be applied to other situations:

- Don't constantly call attention to what we are doing. Worship God, but don't talk about it. If there is a place for self-reflection (and there should be), make it reflection that leads the heart to God, and not back to itself.
- Don't meddle with the historical order of worship. For example, don't put the Lord's Supper before the preaching, thinking that one can prepare for the Word by the Eucharist. Indeed, don't rely on novelty to keep the attention of the congregation. As C. S. Lewis wryly remarked, "I wish they'd remember that the charge to Peter was 'Feed my sheep'; not . . . 'Teach my performing dogs new tricks.'"[11]
- Don't interrupt the service, for example, by putting an announcement or Sunday school skit in the middle of the Communion service proper. (I have seen this done between the Lord's Prayer and the prayer over the bread, for example.)
- Allow for quiet prior to the service.
- Prepare the children (and teachers) if they are to receive the Lord's Supper. Either include them in the preparatory prayers of the congregation, or prepare them before they rejoin the congregation from Church School. Signal the holiness of the Reading of the Word, too, by prayer, action, and song. Show by your actions that these things are holy.
- Allow time for quiet after the Reading of the Word, and during Communion. Resist the temptation to create a particular mood in the congregation by the use of the right music or readings. Rely instead on the Holy Spirit. Do not impose exuberant music upon those who are still reverently receiving the Eucharist.

---

11. C. S. Lewis, *Letters to Malcolm: Chiefly on Prayer* (San Diego: Harvest, 2002) 3.

In the end, we want to treasure the wonder of God-with-us without devolving into an unreal world that presumes we are already complete. We want to take seriously the universal command of the One whom we love: "What I say to you, I say to all: 'Watch'" (Mark 13:37). And, in all our preparation, let us remember that this, too, is the work of God: "Lord, you have heard the desire of the humble: you *will* prepare their heart" (Ps 10:17). If we will just get our agendas and our presuppositions out of the way!

> O Lord God of Abraham, Isaac, and of Israel, our fathers, keep this for ever in the imagination of the thoughts of the heart of your people, and prepare their heart unto You. (1 Chr 29:18)

FOUR

The Future of the Liturgy: A Pentecostal Contribution

Simon Chan

Introduction

In the early 1980s, Robert Webber noticed a number of Evangelicals moving along the Canterbury Trail. Over the years more have followed their lead, not only on the Canterbury Trail, but also the Vatican and the Constantinople Trails. It is not the case that these Christians are getting bored with their own churches. The ancient ways seem to attract the more theologically informed Evangelicals and charismatics from strongholds like Wheaton College and Oral Roberts University. What we are seeing represents one of the most significant theological developments within the Evangelical-charismatic world since the late twentieth century.

A reason frequently given by these pilgrims is the discovery of the power of liturgical and sacramental worship. Today, interest in sacrament and liturgy can be found in a number of movements within the charismatic-Evangelical world. Perhaps the best known, if somewhat controversial, is the emerging church movement.[1] A less well known group is the "Federal Vision" advocates in conservative Presbyterian denominations like the Presbyterian Church of America and the Orthodox Presbyterian Church. Their vision of the church as a visible, spiritual reality entails a strong doctrine of sacramental efficacy.[2] Another group consists of Baptists who are seeking to recover sacramental life and worship by going back to their Reformed roots.[3] Yet another movement—and in my view, the most interesting—consists of mostly Pentecostal-charismatics who are seeking the convergence of the charismatic, Evangelical, and sacramental streams. There are a number of communions practicing convergence today including The International Communion of the Charismatic Episcopal Church, the Communion of Evangelical Episcopal Churches and its sister church the Communion of Convergence Churches. They consider themselves as fully-fledged "communions" with episcopal orders and liturgical worship. The ICCEC and CEEC use an adapted version of the 1979 Prayer Book.[4] All these movements have one thing in common: they have come to the conclusion that their previous emphasis on Evangelical preaching or Pentecostal experience in their worship was inadequate; they now realize that true worship must be ordered around the liturgical celebration of word *and* sacrament.[5]

Now, it is possible that the attraction of the liturgical tradition could be due to the "routinization of charisma" that happens in all religious movements after passing through the initial enthusiastic phase.[6] What used to be a vibrant reality could become familiar and predictable. But what happened to Evangelicals and Pentecostals could also happen to

---

1. For an introduction to the emerging churches, see Eddie Gibbs and Ryan K. Bolger, *Emerging Churches: Creating Christian Community in Postmodern Cultures* (Grand Rapids: Baker, 2005).

2. A good introduction to Federal Vision can be found in Steve Wilkins and Duane Garner, eds., *The Federal Vision* (Monroe, LA: Athanasius, 2004).

3. E.g. Anthony R. Cross and Philip E. Thompson, eds., *Baptist Sacramentalism* (Carlisle: Paternoster, 2003).

4. See their websites: International Communion of the Charismatic Episcopal Church: http://www.iccec.org/; Communion of Evangelical Episcopal Churches: http://www.theceec.org/whoweare.html.

5. For a fuller discussion of these movements, see my article, "New Directions in Evangelical Spirituality," *Journal of Spiritual Formation and Soul Care* 2:2 (2009) 219–37.

6. The "routinization of charisma" was theorized by Max Weber in *The Theory of Social and Economic Organization* (Oxford: Oxford University Press, 1947) 363–86.

sacramentalists. In the mid-1970s, Anglicans in Singapore, having grown weary of their ritualistic worship, began to embrace the charismatic renewal with almost total abandon. In other words, the routinization of charisma is at best a partial explanation.

The phenomenon Webber describes is due to something that goes much deeper. Webber tells us why these "trails" have become attractive to Evangelicals. The Evangelical movement has developed into a system in which faith is equated with belief in certain ideas about God, and worship is equated with indoctrination and evangelism. But Evangelicals are discovering in liturgical worship and the sacraments the means to a fresh and genuine encounter with the awesome and mysterious God.[7] In other words, the attraction of Canterbury is symptomatic of a deep awareness that the ancient liturgy provides certain *norms* of worship and spirituality that are not available in current forms of Evangelical spirituality.

If the problem in Evangelical-charismatic circles is simply a matter of spiritual fatigue or boredom, then all that is needed is a "revival," just like a boring marriage may be pepped up with a romantic cruise to the Caribbean! But most of those on the ancient trails tell us that *that* was not their problem. They were not looking for something to give them a new spiritual uplift; they were looking for something deeper, something that they could not have found within the Evangelical and Pentecostal-charismatic traditions. In short, they have discovered that their own traditions are somewhat incomplete even at their best and that their spiritualities are only a part of something bigger—the Great Tradition. This is probably the most important conclusion that modern Evangelicals and Pentecostals could have ever drawn. This realization, however, does not mean the end of Evangelicalism or Pentecostalism, but it does mean the end of Evangelicalism and Pentecostalism as separate streams of spirituality. Henceforth, they must find their fulfillment within the Great Tradition. It is when they "lose" themselves in the Great Tradition that they will discover their true Evangelical and Pentecostal distinctiveness: "Whoever loses his life will find it" (Matt 16:25).

The coming of Evangelicals and Pentecostals into the liturgical churches, however, has not left the latter unaffected. It has initiated a process that could greatly revitalize the liturgy, which could all too easily sink into ritualism when it is isolated from the Evangelical and charismatic

---

7. Robert E. Webber, *The Younger Evangelicals: Facing the Challenges of the New World* (Grand Rapids: Baker, 2002) 187–204.

streams of spirituality. As the three streams converge, a truly *living* tradition emerges, a tradition characterized by Evangelical commitment to the gospel and Pentecostal openness to the continuing work of the Holy Spirit; that is to say, a liturgy open to doctrinal development[8] since the Spirit is "the power of the future."[9] The gospel story is open to the future because the End toward which the Spirit is leading the church is "not yet." The key is the Spirit who sustains the church in her characteristically "already" and "not yet" eschatological existence.

This paper focuses on the Pentecostal contribution to a revitalized liturgy because a Pentecostal perspective, as we shall see, provides a fuller account of the gospel story enacted in the ancient liturgy.[10]

Pentecostal Sacramentality

The fact that there are a number of Evangelical-charismatic movements seeking to incorporate themselves into the sacramental tradition is proof that these traditions are not as incompatible as they were once thought to be. This is, surprisingly, even more true of Pentecostals than Evangelicals. The disorderly "enthusiasm" of Pentecostals is often thought to be so far removed from the solemn and predictable liturgy that "never the twain shall meet." The fact of the matter is that Pentecostals are far more sacramental than they themselves realize. In the dialogues between Catholics and Pentecostals, Pentecostal theologian Howard Ervin observes that there is "an intuitive awareness of sacramental realities in the Pentecostal experience" in their practice of tongues and healing.[11] The sacramental nature of Pentecostal faith can be seen in the way Pentecostals understand

---

8. Doctrinal development is to be distinguished from innovation or novelty. Novelty, as the ancient theologians reminded us, is heresy, whereas the living tradition is rooted in the story of the triune God so that whatever is "new" grows out of "the old, old story."

9. See, e.g., Robert Jenson, *Systematic Theology I: The Triune God* (Oxford: Oxford University Press, 1997) 146–61 *passim*.

10. I am mindful of the fact that, according to Paul Bradshaw, the Christian liturgy became more homogenized around the Paschal mystery only in the fourth century. But what is interesting is that there is such a process of standardization. See Paul F. Bradshaw, "The Homogenization of the Christian Liturgy—Ancient and Modern: Presidential Address," *Studia Liturgica* 26 (1996) 1–15. Cf. the following article by Irmgard Pahl, "The Paschal Mystery in its Central Meaning for the Shape of Christian Liturgy," 16–38.

11. Veli-Matti Kärkkäinen, *Spiritus ubi vult spirat: Pneumatology in Roman Catholic-Pentecostal Dialogue (1972-1989)* (Helsinki: Luther Agricola Society, 1998) 273.

their central experience of Spirit-baptism to be signaled by the *physical* act of speaking in tongues: the physical points to and conveys the spiritual.[12]

Many Pentecostals have applied this sense of sacramentality especially to the Lord's Supper even though they still prefer to call baptism and the Lord's Supper "ordinances." The Lord's Supper is more than a memorial. An early Pentecostal, P. C. Nelson, whose *Bible Doctrines* has nurtured cohorts of students in Pentecostal Bible institutes throughout the world, refers to the Lord's Supper in this way:

> The Lord's Supper is a healing ordinance. If you are sick or afflicted in your body and can discern the healing virtue in the body of our Lord, typified by the bread, you may receive healing and strength for your body as well as for your spiritual nature.[13]

Outside the West, Pentecostal sacramentality is even more evident. The research of Harold Turner, Allan Anderson, and others have noted the widespread use of physical objects for spiritual ends: anointing oil, anointed cloth, holy water, and various physical objects for healing and exorcism.[14] One explanation for this phenomenon, according to Turner, is that Pentecostals especially in Asia and Africa share a deep affinity with the sacramental worldview found in primal religions.[15] More recently, a number of prominent Pentecostal-charismatics have highlighted the importance of the Lord's Supper as a means of grace. William L. De Arteaga, a priest of the Communion of Evangelical Episcopal Churches, has argued that major revivals in the past have been built on the central observance of the Lord's Supper.[16] Swedish charismatic Ulf Ekmann believes that communion is "a means to a more powerful spiritual life and . . . more

---

12. E.g., Frank D. Macchia, "Groans Too Deep for Words: Towards A Theology of Tongues as Initial Evidence," *Asian Journal of Pentecostal Studies* 1:2 (1998) 149–73.

13. Cited in Kärkkäinen, *Spiritus ubi vult spirat*, 282. *Bible Doctrines* was first published in 1934.

14. Allan Anderson, *Zion and Pentecost: The Spirituality and Experience of Pentecostal and Zionist/Apostolic Churches in South Africa* (Pretoria: University of South Africa Press, 2000) 290–300; "African Initiated Churches of the Spirit and Pneumatology," *Word and World* 23 (2003) 178–86. Cf. Philip Jenkins, *The Next Christendom: The Coming of Global Christianity* (Oxford: Oxford University Press, 2007); *The New Faces of Christianity: Believing the Bible in the Global South* (Oxford: Oxford University Press, 2006).

15. Harold Turner, *The Roots of Science: An Investigative Journey through the World's Religions* (Auckland: The Deep Sight Trust, 1998) 142.

16. William L. De Arteaga, *Forgotten Power: The Significance of the Lord's Supper in Revival* (Grand Rapids: Zondervan, 2002).

intimate fellowship with Jesus."[17] Singapore mega-church pastor Joseph Prince speaks of the consumption of the broken body of Christ in quasi-magical terms when he encourages his members to have private communion as frequently as possible to ensure good health: "... if you are sick, I would recommend that you have Communion daily.... I know of people who are so radical that they take it like medicine—three times a day.... They get radical results."[18]

There are many fads in the Pentecostal-charismatic movement, but the recovery of the sacramental dimension of worship is not one of them; rather, it reflects something that is deeply embedded in the Pentecostal spiritual consciousness. Its recovery could be explained by the fact that in their ecumenical engagements, Pentecostals are discovering the conceptual tools to make explicit what has hitherto been implicit in their experience. Their theology of the Lord's Supper may sound crude and is often expressed in highly individualistic terms, but there is no denying that they have discovered from experience something real and life-transforming.

Theological Basis of Pentecostal Sacramentality

If Pentecostals share a "deep affinity" with primal religions, as noted by Turner above, this fact provides only a partial explanation for Pentecostal sacramentality. Theologically, Pentecostalism is *practically* rooted in the trinitarian economy especially with respect to the third Person, and it is from this pneumatological foundation that Pentecostal spirituality can be properly understood. Pentecostals have always understood their distinctive faith and experience in relation to the Pentecost event as recorded in Acts 2. But they had understood this relation intuitively rather than reflectively.[19] They had rightly grasped the paradigmatic nature of the Pentecost event for the people of God, but they lacked the theological language to explicate it fully. Thus what comes through their songs, popular sermons, and testimonies was a sense of the personal presence of Jesus Christ through the presence and power of the Holy Spirit.[20] No attempt

---

17. Ulf Ekmann, *Take, Eat—A Book on Holy Communion* (n.p., 2006) 4.

18. Joseph Prince, *Health and Wholeness through the Holy Communion* (Singapore: 22 Media, 2006) 45.

19. Here is an example of *lex orandi* giving rise to *lex credendi*.

20. E.g., Steven Land, *Pentecostal Spirituality: A Passion for the Kingdom* (Sheffield, UK: Sheffield Academic Press, 1993).

was made to explain Jesus' relation to the Spirit—not, at least, until they had to confront the "new issue" brought on by Oneness Pentecostals who explicitly denied the Trinity.[21] But even that explanation only grounds the trinitarian Pentecostals in traditional trinitarian theology but does not quite spell out a distinctive *Pentecostal* trinitarian theology.

Our task is to make explicit what was for the most part grasped instinctively in Pentecostalism. Theologically, Pentecost could be said to be the event in which the full trinitarian nature of God is revealed. The trinitarian narrative centers in two climactic events commonly referred to as "the two sendings" (cf. Gal 4:4-6). The story could be first glimpsed in the accounts of the New Testament where Jesus is clearly distinguished from the Father as the one sent from the Father, yet he possesses qualities which unmistakably identify him with the God of Israel.[22] The close identification of Jesus Christ with Yahweh of the Old Testament was such as to force the early Christians to qualify their inherited monotheism. But while the coming of Jesus Christ "complicates" Jewish monotheism, it is not the end of the story. The story continues to unfold with the account of the second sending, i.e., the sending of the Holy Spirit. This second sending, especially as it is explicated in the Farewell Discourse (John 14–16), reveals for the first time the distinct identity of the Spirit, as the "other Comforter."[23] The Spirit cannot truly be the "other" Comforter of the same kind as Jesus if he is not also fully a divine person as Jesus is. What is perhaps most significant in the Farewell Discourse is that this revelation of the Holy Spirit as the third person is explicitly linked to his coming to indwell the church.[24] It is in connection with his indwelling the church that the Holy Spirit is revealed as the third person of the Trinity. This is why, historically, the Spirit is always spoken of in connection with the church, e.g., the Creed links the church to the third article of the creed.

---

21. For a definitive account of the "new issue" see David A. Reed, *"In Jesus' Name: The History and Beliefs of Oneness Pentecostals* (Blandford Forum, Dorset: Deo, 2008).

22. See, e.g., N. T. Wright, *The Challenge of Jesus* (London: SPCK, 2000) 91–92. Cf. *The New Testament and the People of God* (Minneapolis: Fortress, 1992) 362.

23. See e.g. Raymond E. Brown, *The Gospel According to John*, The Anchor Bible 2 (Garden City, NY: Doubleday, 1970) 1139.

24. Cf. James Dunn, "Towards the Spirit of Christ: The Emergence of the Distinctive Features of Christian Pneumatology," in *The Word of the Spirit: Pneumatology and Pentecostalism*, ed. Michael Welker (Grand Rapids: Eerdmans, 2006) 12–13.

In the Canons of Hippolytus, the question posed to catechumens at their baptism was: "Do you believe in the Holy Spirit *in* the holy church?"[25]

In this all-too-brief description of the trinitarian economy, we see that the work of the Spirit is utterly determinative of the church. Theologically, we cannot even begin to talk about ecclesiology without reference to pneumatology.[26] The relationship between ecclesiology and pneumatology may be summed up as follows: The church is defined by its relation to the Spirit, and the Spirit is revealed as the third person in the economy of salvation in relation to his coming to indwell the church.[27]

The coming of the Spirit to indwell the church constitutes the foundation of Christian worship which begins with the church's grateful acknowledgement of God as Father: "Because you are sons, God sent the Spirit of his Son into our hearts, the Spirit who calls out, 'Abba, Father'" (Gal 4:6). His coming into the church awakens the filial instinct to pray: "Our Father who art in heaven . . . ." Worship is the Spirit-inspired response of God's people to the revelation of the triune God. His indwelling the church is what makes a gathering of ordinary people into the body of Christ and the temple of the Spirit in which praise is continually offered to God as Father. This doxological theme is schematized in the church's liturgy which enacts the Paschal Mystery (the first sending) and seeks to actualize what the Spirit is doing in the church through its core practices (the second sending).[28] These core practices are not invented by the church, but are ordained by Christ himself and "mirror" Christ.[29] They are constitutive of the church just as the Spirit's work is constitutive of the church. Therefore, they could be considered the works of the Spirit, that is, the means by which the Spirit works to constitute the church as church. In other words, if the liturgy *is* the work of the Spirit, then the whole liturgical

---

25. Hippolytus *The Apostolic Tradition* 21.17.

26. Ralph del Colle, e.g., refers to ecclesiology as a branch of pneumatology. See *Christ and the Spirit: Spirit-Christology in Trinitarian Perspective* (Oxford: Oxford University Press, 1994) 25.

27. For a succinct discussion of the "mutuality" of the Spirit and church, see Nikos A. Nissiotis, "Spirit, Church, and Ministry," *Theology Today* 19 (1963) 484–99.

28. For a study of the church's constitutive core practices, see Reinhard Hütter, *Suffering Divine Things: Theology as Christian Practice* (Grand Rapids: Eerdmans, 2000). See also David L. Stubbs, "Practices, Core Practices, and the Work of the Spirit," *Journal for Christian Theological Research* 9 (2004) 23. Stubbs notes that the liturgy is not only the work *of* the people but also work *for* the people. The liturgy is where both the people are doing the work *of* God and the Spirit is at work *for* the people.

29. Stubbs, "Practices," 23–24.

celebration, in the words of Nikos Nissiotis, is a "perpetual Pentecost."[30] It is the celebration of the Paschal Mystery in the power of the Holy Spirit. Although different Christian traditions have identified different constitutive core practices, two core practices have always been affirmed: word and sacraments. These have come to constitute the normative form and content of the liturgy in most Christian traditions today.

The identification of the liturgy of word and sacrament as the work of the Spirit, however, carries certain attendant dangers, namely, the temptation to domesticate the Spirit and thus to make the church and its special class of priests the dispenser of grace. The church is all too familiar with these dangers.[31] How then are we to identify the core practices as the works of the Holy Spirit without succumbing to the sinful desire to domesticate the Holy Spirit? The answer is to be found in the fact that the church exists in *epicletic* relationship to the Spirit. This is the distinctive contribution of Eastern Orthodoxy.

The Spirit comes to indwell the church, but is not the church's possession. Rather, by regularly invoking the Holy Spirit, the church recognizes its total dependence on the Spirit to constitute it anew. This means that the church is primarily an *event* of the Spirit and only secondarily an institution.[32] Zizioulas, for example, insists that we must not only see the Spirit as *having come* to indwell the church, but also as *always coming* from "beyond" history to transform ordinary things into "charismatic-Pentecostal events."[33] Each time the church gathers to celebrate the liturgy, it is being constituted anew by the Spirit.

The Pentecostal Contribution

However, the Orthodox understanding of the church's *epicletic* relation to the Spirit, while true in principle, may not always be true in practice. Here

---

30. Nissiotis, "Called to Unity," 54. Cf. Alexander Schmemann, *For the Life of the World: Sacraments and Orthodoxy* (Crestwood, NY: St. Vladimir Seminary Press, 2000) 27.

31. It should be said that charismatics could be just as guilty of manipulating the Spirit as sacramentalists, for instance, when they speak of "praise" as a means to bring down the presence of God.

32. John D. Zizioulas, "The Doctrine of the Trinity Today: Suggestions for Ecumenical Study," in *The Forgotten Trinity*, ed. Alasdair Herond (London: British Council of churches, 1991) 27–28.

33. John D. Zizioulas, *Being as Communion: Studies in Personhood and the Church* (Crestwood, NY: St. Vladimir Seminary Press, 1993) 113–16.

is where Pentecostals could make their distinctive contribution to the liturgical tradition. They too recognize the church as a Spirit-constituted event, but they back up their belief with a *practical* pneumatology.[34] Pentecostals may not talk about the *epiclesis*, but their practice certainly acknowledges the *epicletic* orientation of the church. In their worship the person of the Spirit is frequently invoked, as exemplified in this old Pentecostal hymn by Charles H. Gabriel (1912):

> Lord, as of old at Pentecost/Thou didst thy pow'r display,/With cleansing, purifying flame/Descend on us today.
>
> Refrain:
>
> Lord, send the old-time pow'r,/ the Pentecostal pow'r!/Thy floodgates of blessing on us throw open wide/Lord, send the old-time pow'r,/ the Pentecostal pow'r/That sinners be converted and thy name glorified!
>
> All self consume, all sin destroy!/With earnest zeal endue/Each waiting heart to work for Thee;/O Lord, our faith renew!
>
> Speak, Lord! Before thy throne we wait,/Thy promise we believe,/ And will not let thee go until/The blessing we receive.[35]

They may not use the "Veni Creator" in their prayers, but the Holy Spirit is often called upon to heal the sick and empower the saints in their spiritual battles. Cho Yonggi, pastor of the world's largest Pentecostal congregation, even encourages Christians to cultivate fellowship *with* the Spirit. According to Cho, the Holy Spirit is like the senior business partner with whom we must actively consult if we hope to succeed in our endeavors.[36] Although, as I have pointed out elsewhere, there is a danger of over-individualizing the Spirit in such talks,[37] yet the use of such a hyperbole serves at least to remind us that the Holy Spirit is always above us, always coming from beyond; he "does not 'become' history, but works

---

34. The only difficulty is that Pentecostals fail to give due weight to the institutional character of the church, and consequently end up with a rather unstable ecclesiastical structure.

35. *Melodies of Praise* (Springfield, MO: Gospel House, 1957) #53. Public domain.

36. *The Holy Spirit, My Senior Partner* (Altamonte Springs: Creation House, 1989).

37. Simon Chan, "The Pneumatology of David Yonggi Cho," in *David Yonggi Cho: A Close Look at His Theology and Ministry*, eds. Wonsuk Ma, William W. Menzies and Hyeon-sung Bae (Baguio, Philippines: APTS, 2004) 95–120.

'on' history from the future."[38] The Holy Spirit cannot be domesticated by our liturgy, but rather comes to enliven the liturgy.

Epiclesis in the West

But how much of the Western liturgy acknowledges the *epicletic* existence of the church? Here, I would like to make two observations. First, although the pneumatological dimension of the church and of the sacrament is widely acknowledged since Vatican II, the *epiclesis* does not seem to play as prominent a role as in the East.[39] The traditional Western liturgical practice seems to favor bracketing the pneumatological within the Christological. We see this in the modern Roman Missal. Of the four eucharistic prayers, only one (no. 4) contains an *epiclesis*, and even here the words of institution are central in that they form the culmination of the eucharistic prayer. The same order is found in the four eucharistic prayers in the ASB. The 1979 prayer book of ECUSA (now TEC) has the *epiclesis* follow the words of institution. But the *epiclesis* is not emphatically pneumatological.[40] More recent Western eucharistic prayers have sought to correct the imbalance. This is reflected in *Common Worship* (2000) where, of the eight eucharistic prayers, four culminate with the *epiclesis* (D, F, G, H) and the others with the words of institution (A, B, C, E). In the East, the eucharistic prayer always culminates with the *epiclesis*, thus clearly distinguishing the pneumatological from the Christological dimensions within the trinitarian pattern of the "two sendings."[41] This pattern is followed in the newer communion rituals of mainline Protestant

---

38. Jerry Zenon Skira, "Christ, the Spirit and the Church in Modern Orthodox Theology: A Comparison of Georges Florovsky, Vladimir Lossky, Nikos Nissiotis and John Zizioulas," PhD diss., University of Toronto, 1998, 181. Skira is referring to Zizioulas' pneumatology. Cf. Zizioulas, *Being as Communion*, 130.

39. The theologian most responsible for the rediscovery of the *epiclesis* in the Catholic Church is probably Yves Congar. See Isaac Kizhakkeparampil, *The Invocation of the Holy Spirit as Constitutive of the Sacraments according to Cardinal Yves Congar* (Rome: Gregorian University Press, 1995).

40. Rite 1: ". . . vouchsafe to bless and sanctify with thy *Word and Spirit*, these thy gifts and creatures of bread and wine. Rite 2: ". . . with thy *Word and Spirit*, to bless and sanctify these gifts of bread and wine . . ." Cf. Cranmer's revised mass of 1549: "With *Thy Holy Spirit and Word* vouchsafe to bless and sanctify these Thy gifts and creatures of Bread and Wine" (emphasis added).

41. See the Divine Liturgy of St. John Chrysostom.

denominations like the United Methodist Church and the Evangelical Lutheran Church of America.[42]

Second, the subordinate role of the Spirit in the liturgy can be seen in the place given to prayers for healing in the liturgy. While the special actions of the Spirit to bring wholeness and healing to body and mind are acknowledged, prayers for healing are not a *regular* part of the central liturgical celebration of the church, but are consigned to the occasional healing services. This is true of *Common Worship* as well as the Roman Missal. In the Roman church, prayers for healing, whether liturgical or non-liturgical, are explicitly excluded from the regular mass and the liturgy of the hours.[43] This is despite the fact that some recent Catholic writings have recognized the close connection between healing and communion.[44] If prayer for healing is found in the mass it is only as part of the general intercession. The rationale is that the regular mass is intended to "bring the faithful to recognize in the Eucharist the wonderful presence of Christ and to invite them to a spiritual union with him, a union which finds its culmination in sacramental Communion."[45] Here again we see a preference for the Christological over the pneumatological dimensions of the church. This tendency to marginalize the church's *epicletic* relationship to the Spirit raises a number of questions:

- If the liturgy is indeed the event of the Spirit in which the church is being actualized anew, should we not give greater prominence to this fact?
- Should we be satisfied only with the *institutional* character of the church and not also the constitutive *event* of the Spirit?
- If the work of the Spirit in the church is to bring wholeness and unity in the body of Christ, should prayers for healing be confined only to special or occasional healing services? Shouldn't this perennial need of the church be more clearly reflected in the regular liturgy?

42. See the *United Methodist Book of Worship* (Nashville: United Methodist Publishing House, 1992) and the *Evangelical Lutheran Worship* (Minneapolis: Augsburg Fortress, 2006). Previous communion rituals of these denominations do not have an *epiclesis*.

43. "Instruction on Prayers for Healing." See under Disciplinary Norms, Art. 7, §1 and 3. Online: http://www.vatican.va/roman_curia/congregations/cfaith/documents/rc_con_cfaith_doc_20001123_istruzione_en.html.

44. See, e.g., John H. Hampsch, *The Healing Power of the Eucharist* (Ann Arbor, MI: Servant, 1999).

45. "Instruction on Prayers for Healing," no. 5.

- If we believe that the Holy Spirit is not only in history but also comes from "beyond" history, where is the place in the liturgy where the "beyondness" of the Spirit is actually recognized?
- If the whole liturgy is the work of the Spirit, should the *epiclesis* be confined only to the eucharistic prayer over the bread and wine? Should there not be other places where the Spirit is explicitly invoked?

Perhaps we need to inject an Orthodox-Pentecostal synthesis into the Western liturgical tradition if it is to maintain its ancient trajectory into the future under the guidance of the Holy Spirit. This could be done in several ways.

First, the Western liturgical tradition perhaps needs some stronger input from the pneumatological emphases of Orthodoxy and the practical pneumatology of Pentecostalism. It needs to give more room for the Holy Spirit to move especially in the regular liturgy. I want to stress the *regular* liturgy because the Holy Spirit should not be thought of as functioning only on special occasions. There is a place for special services, but wholeness of body, mind, and spirit should not be thought of as occasional matters. There is no reason why the ministry of healing, for instance, should not be a part of the "ordinary" of the Sunday liturgy. Praying regularly for healing and wholeness does not imply that God must always heal physically; rather, it is to recognize that our broken bodies and spirits are symptomatic of the body of Christ that is still in a state of brokenness and that this fragmented body is an eschatological community anticipating the new creation. The prayer for healing points to a much bigger problem, namely, the current fragmentation of the church; but it also reveals a transcendent hope, namely, the overcoming of our present fragmentation in the fellowship and unity of the Holy Spirit. In short, there is an intimate connection between healing and the church's catholicity. As Geoffrey Wainwright has rightly pointed out, healing is the fruit of catholicity.[46] Perhaps healing should also be seen as the *means* of catholicity.

Second, the church's *epicletic* relation to the Spirit could be enlarged if we follow the example in the Wesleyan tradition of seeing the Communion as a "converting ordinance." Wesley allowed the Lord's Supper to be given to baptized members who did not yet have a specific "conversion" experience precisely so that they might have such an experience. In early Wesleyan

---

46. Geoffrey Wainwright, *Worship with One Accord: Where Liturgy and Ecumenism Embrace* (Oxford: Oxford University Press, 1997) 7.

meetings, sometimes dramatic experiences accompanied the communion service. We read of a number of such accounts in John Wesley's journal: "Many were cut to the heart, and at the Lord's Supper many were wounded and many healed."[47] As De Arteaga has shown in his history of sacramental revivals, things *do* happen at the Lord's Supper when there is an expectation that the Holy Spirit is present to do his work among God's people. Such expectations are often absent when the primary focus is on Holy Communion as an *anamnetic* event. The concentration is more on remembering what Christ did than in anticipating the action of the Spirit in the here and now—the Spirit who is the "firstfruits" of the new creation. In short, the Western eucharistic theology is solidly Christological but not sufficiently pneumatological. The result is that its eucharistic observance does not raise very high expectations that the Spirit will do "surprising works" among us. By contrast, the Wesleys had a very different expectation at the Lord's Supper: it is an occasion when the Holy Spirit will, in the words of one Wesleyan hymn, "realize the sign":

> Come, Holy Ghost, thine influence shed,/And realize the sign;/
> Thy life infuse into the bread,/Thy power into the wine.[48]

Today, it is mostly the Pentecostal-charismatics who are demonstrating that the eucharist as an *epicletic* event has practical consequences.[49]

Third, the invocation of the Holy Spirit should not be confined to the bread and wine. The *whole* liturgy sustains an *epicletic* relation to the Spirit.[50] This means that there should be other places in the liturgy where the Spirit is invoked. Besides the prayer for healing and wholeness, space could be given for prayers for the fresh gifts of the Spirit to be bestowed; for a new in-filling of the Holy Spirit in line with Eph 5:18; for the illumination of the Spirit before the word is read and preached; for the church to be made one in "the fellowship of the Holy Spirit"; etc. But Pentecostals do more than just pray; they act out their prayer. Prayer for a fresh in-filling of the Spirit is often carried out in the context of the "altar

---

47. John Wesley, *Journal*, 20 July 1777, in *The Works of John Wesley*, Vol. IV, 3rd ed. (Grand Rapids: Baker, 1986).

48. Franklin Whaling, ed., *John and Charles Wesley: Selected Writings and Hymns*, in Classics of Western Spirituality (New York: Paulist, 1981) 260.

49. See De Arteaga, *Forgotten Power*, 237ff.

50. See Alexander Schmemann, *The Eucharist: Sacrament of the Kingdom*, trans. Paul Kachur (Crestwood, NY: St. Vladimir Seminary Press, 2003) 222.

ministry." The fellowship of the Spirit is seen in various forms of tactile expressions including holding hands, hugging, etc. The Holy Spirit manifests himself in very concrete ways, and this is reflected in the strongly kinesthetic dimensions of worship.[51]

The convergence of the Pentecostal and the liturgical traditions will be mutually enriching. The liturgical tradition will attain a fuller understanding of the church as the temple of the Spirit when the *epiclesis* comes to play a more prominent role. At the same time, the Pentecostal tradition will be enriched when the dynamic works of the Spirit are understood within the liturgical context. Take the matter of divine healing. Pentecostal-charismatics have tended to see healing as a blessing given to individuals. But when healing is understood and practiced within the liturgy, the primary concern is no longer my own personal well being, but the total well being of the body of Christ of which I am a member. Physical healing is only an aspect of the larger work of the Spirit of bringing wholeness (catholicity) to the entire body by effecting deeper unity with Christ, the head, and unity with one another.

Conclusion

I began by referring to Webber's *Evangelicals on the Canterbury Trail* to point out that the liturgical tradition has much to offer Evangelicals and Pentecostals. At the same time, those in the liturgical tradition need to remember that Evangelicals and charismatics are embracing the liturgy not to find a *substitute* but a solid *anchor* for their Evangelical and charismatic heritage. They are looking for convergence of the three spiritual streams. The basically liturgical structure of worship cannot but be enriched by Evangelical fidelity and Pentecostal vitality. The future of the liturgy is only as hopeful as convergence is seriously pursued.

---

51. See, e.g., Daniel E. Albrecht, *Rites in the Spirit: A Ritual Approach to Pentecostal/Charismatic Spirituality*, JPT Supplement (Sheffield, UK: Sheffield Academic Press, 1999) 147–48.

FIVE

Community: To What End?

D. Stephen Long

After an outdoor sermon was delivered by the Anglican priest, Mr. John Wesley, a number of persons were moved and approached him, asking what they should do to be saved. His response was (and I paraphrase), "Meet me next Thursday and I'll put you in a small group." He did not ask anyone to pray the sinner's prayer. Never did he say, "With every eye closed and every head bowed, let me see a hand." Evangelism, and for that matter salvation, was not for Mr. Wesley a private or individual event; it was communal. "Christianity," he once wrote, "is a social religion." And by that he did not mean, as it is often wrongly interpreted, that Christians should be involved in the public sphere or work for social justice; he meant something more specific. Wesley wrote, "I shall endeavor to show that Christianity is essentially a social religion, and that to turn it into a solitary relation is indeed to destroy it . . . Secondly, that to conceal this religion is impossible."[1]

Wesley makes two claims here. First, Christianity is not about a solitary, individual relation with God, but can only rightly be understood

---

1. John Wesley, *The Works of John Wesley* (Grand Rapids: Baker, 1996) I.1:533.

as "communal." Second, the communal character of Christianity cannot but be a public witness. I would like to explain both these points and then conclude with how Wesley's very traditional understanding of the communal character of Christianity contributed to the ministry of the Church of the Redeemer at Northwestern University.

"Christianity is essentially a social religion"

Christianity as a social religion only makes sense because of the way of life Jesus proclaimed as blessed. Wesley makes this statement in the context of his interpretation of the Sermon on the Mount. The beatitudes give us the end or purpose for community. In fact, they exhibited what Wesley meant by his well-known expression, "religion of the heart." He did not mean some private existential experience about which no one can judge. He meant a social reality, embodied in the community of faith, that once embodied could not be concealed. Here he is in touch with a central theme in Christian tradition, which can be found in a number of church Fathers as well as saints and doctors, especially St. Augustine and Thomas Aquinas. It is a theme that has disappeared in much of contemporary Christian ethics. The theme is this: Jesus' pronouncement of beatitude in the Sermon on the Mount sets forth the end or purpose of the Christian life. It discloses to us true happiness, which is communal.

Anyone who has studied the history of ethics knows that for many ancient ethicists the true end of life was happiness. Every action aimed to make one happy explicitly or implicitly. Nearly all early Christians found what Robert Wilken called "a serendipitous congruence of the Bible and the wisdom of the Greeks and Romans" with respect to this life of beatitude.[2] (Not all contemporary Christians do; Nicholas Wolterstorff, for instance, does not.) Yet Christians made significant revisions to the ancient understanding. The happiness Aristotle envisioned could not be found solely in immanent, natural human powers, but only in an eschatological promise that comes in the middle of time through the way of life Jesus called "blessed." When Mr. Wesley speaks of the "religion of the heart," he does not mean some existential experience of absolute dependence, or a momentary transaction between God and the individual

---

2. Robert Wilken, *The Spirit of Early Christian Thought: Seeking the Face of God* (New Haven, CT: Yale University Press, 2003) 273.

sinner. He means the life of beatitude Jesus announced, especially the first seven beatitudes: poverty of spirit, meekness, mournfulness, righteousness (or justice), mercifulness, purity of heart, and peaceableness. He also thought, as did Augustine and Aquinas, that anyone who truly embodied these seven virtues would most likely receive the eighth: "persecution for righteousness sake."

Why did these beatitudes require that Christianity be a "social religion"? We can see this in Wesley's explanation of the beatitude of "meekness," of which he writes, "As it implies mildness, gentleness and long-suffering, it cannot possibly have a being . . . without an intercourse with other men. . . . So that to attempt turning this into a solitary virtue is to destroy it from the face of the earth."[3] The true embodiment of a life of beatitude requires living in proximity with others, seeking the same end.

That people bound together communally seeking the same end will bring happiness runs counter to most everything we moderns hold near and dear. Most of the aphorisms by which we are encouraged to live suggest exactly the opposite: "Think for yourself"; "Be an individual"; "An army of one"; "What is a man, what has he got, if not himself then he has not"; "I took a chance I did it my way"; "If Billy jumped off a cliff/bridge . . . ?" "Think outside the box"; "Affirm diversity, pluralism, etc." But for both Scripture and Christian tradition, the modern emphasis on the individual who stands against the community asserting his or her own independence is nothing short of a life of idiocy. We see this in the famous Acts passages in chapters 2 and 4 which extol a life lived in common: "They held all things in common (*koina*) (Acts 2:44), and no one said that what he possessed was his own (*idion*) but all things were common" (*koina*). Here we find a contrast between a life in common (*koina*) with a life lived as if it were its own (*idion*). The word individual and idiot both come from this same Greek word—*idion*.

Wesley stated Christianity is a social religion because he recognized that the pursuit and embodiment of the Christian life, primarily attested in the Sermon on the Mount, was not a life that could be accomplished by heroic individuals nor exercised by solitary persons. It requires life in community. How are we to pursue and embody meekness, mercifulness, peaceableness, righteousness, or justice without living truthfully with others who will help us name our own self-deceptions about such gifts?

---

3. Wesley, *Works*, §I.3, 1:534.

Wesley was on to something here when he insisted that salvation doesn't occur primarily with individuals standing alone, but with people bound together in a common life.

"Secondly, that to conceal this religion is impossible"[4]

Intrinsic to this community's way of life is its witness. Evangelism and mission are not strategies one can implement using the latest sociological analyses. Evangelism is the life of faithfulness. This is the basis of Wesley's second statement—"to conceal this religion is impossible."[5] The common life, the life of communion, lived in the midst of various and diverse cities cannot but be a visible and public witness to all the inhabitants of those cities. This too emerges from Jesus' teaching on the Sermon on the Mount. "You are a city set on a hill . . . ." (Matt 5:14). The end of Christian community is to be a city set in the midst of the cities bearing witness to the city that is coming (Revelation 21). This of course is also essential to the Christian tradition for it is what generated the Christian mission in the first place. It is the call of Israel, into which we have graciously been grafted, the call not to be like the other nations for the sake of the nations. To fulfill this call, God gave them sacred possessions: the divine name, the Torah, and the Temple. We believe that Christ is the fulfillment of these promises. He bears the divine name, fulfils the law, which is a communication of God's own being, and his body becomes the "Temple," the site of God, which is mediated to us by our communion in Word and sacrament. Christianity's participation in the mission of Israel is what makes it essentially a social religion.

Wesley understood this well. It is why for him the proper relation between law and Gospel was the basis for Christian witness. He stated that there was no contradiction at all between the law and the Gospel. When he first formed the Methodist communities, he gave them three general rules by which they were to live: do no harm, do good, and attend upon the ordinances of God. (Anyone familiar with Aquinas's account of the natural law will see a strong resemblance here: the first two are what he called the first principle of practical reason—do good and avoid evil.) Under each of these rules he placed specific examples, often straight from

---

4. Wesley, *Works*, §I.1, 1:533.
5. Ibid.

the Ten Commandments or other biblical commands. The Methodists were to observe these commands, including the third that called for a common worship life, but Wesley also called these rules nothing more than the "religion of the world" or the "righteousness of a Pharisee."[6] The bare observance of these commands is insufficient, even though that is better than their willful violation. The commands, like the law, have an end, which is the "religion of the heart," the life of beatitude. Wesley feared that the church of his day had the form of religion; it had the law, the creeds, and a proper liturgy, but it lacked the substance—the life of beatitude. He called Christians to gather in a community, bound together by these rules, in order to assist each other in the pursuit of that life of beatitude, which of course always comes as a gift of the Spirit.

When the life of beatitude is communally embodied, it produces a witness that cannot be concealed. This, too, is a common theme in Christian tradition. We find it in the Epistle to Diognetus when the author, whoever he may be, explains the shape of Christian community:

> But, inhabiting Greek as well as barbarian cities, according as the lot of each of them has determined, and following the customs of the natives in respect to clothing, food, and the rest of their ordinary conduct, *they display to us their wonderful and confessedly striking method of life.* They dwell in their own countries, but simply as sojourners. As citizens, they share in all things with others, and yet endure all things as if foreigners. Every foreign land is to them as their native country, and every land of their birth as a land of strangers. They marry, as do all [others]; they beget children; but they do not destroy their offspring. [Literally, "cast away fœtuses."] They have a common table, but not a common bed. They are in the flesh, but they do not live after the flesh. They pass their days on earth, but they are citizens of heaven. They obey the prescribed laws, and at the same time surpass the laws by their lives. They love all men, and are persecuted by all. They are unknown and condemned; they are put to death, and restored to life. They are poor, yet make many rich; they are in lack of all things, and yet abound in all; they are dishonoured, and yet in their very dishonour are glorified.[7]

---

6. Wesley, Sermon 25, "Upon Our Lord's Sermon on the Mount, V," *Works* §IV.7–9, 1:565–67.

7. *Epistle to Diognetus*. Online: http://earlychurchtexts.com/public/epistle_to_diognetus.htm.

If we had time, we could easily trace how this theme of a "common life on display" was prevalent throughout the tradition up until the latter Medieval and early modern eras. As the epistle notes, the common life of the Christian is not an escape, a withdrawal, or sectarian removal from ordinary life. We are found in every city, wearing the dress and eating the food of that city. We still marry and raise children like others. But within these cities, among the diversity of dress, language, food, we nonetheless share a "common table" and offer a "striking method of life." We are a transnational community—a communion—found in every local precinct. This is what it means to be church, and one cannot be Christian without church. It is why Christianity is essentially a social religion.

To be church requires an embodiment of all four marks of the church that we confess each week: unity, catholicity, apostolicity, and holiness. These are the work of the Holy Spirit in our common life. The Catholic theologian, Yves Congar, explained this well. The Spirit, he wrote, "is the extreme communication of God himself, God as grace, God *in us* and, in this sense, God outside himself."[8] The Spirit, then, is the "principle of communion." By "principle" is meant the living, animating force. By "communion" is meant a communication that unites communicator and those communicated. The Spirit communicates with that which is not God—creation—bringing it into unity with God and with each other without losing the distinction between God and creatures. For Congar, as for the Christian tradition, we find communion as communication in the very act of the giving of the Divine Name in Exodus 3. He writes, "Spirit can further God's plan, which can be expressed in the words 'communion,' 'many in one' and 'uniplurality.' At the end there will be a state in which God will be 'everything to everyone' (1 Cor 15: 28). In other words, there will be one life animating many without doing violence to the inner experience of anyone, just as, on Mount Sinai, Yahweh set fire to the bush and it was not consumed."[9] This unity is expressed in catholicity, apostolicity, and holiness, just as each of them is expressed only in the other three.

Catholicity is both particular and universal at the same time. The church is born at Pentecost where each can hear a common, universal proclamation in the singular particularity of one's own language. The

---

8. Yves Congar, *He is Lord and Giver of Life*, vol. 2 of *I Believe in the Holy Spirit* (New York: Crossroad, 1997) 17–18.

9. Ibid., 17.

common and universal is also "apostolic" in that the apostles give us the language of the faith.

That the church is apostolic means that it must always relate to, and therefore be "in conformity with the origins of Christianity." It was the Apostles who witnessed first hand the person and work of Christ. Their witness is primarily attested in Scripture. But because they claim that Christ is both the beginning and the end, the "alpha and omega," apostolicity is not only backward looking; it is also forward looking, anticipating the end. Therefore Congar writes, "Apostolicity is the mark that for the Church is both a gift of grace and a task. It makes the Church fill the space between the Alpha and Omega by ensuring that there is a continuity between the two and a substantial identity between the end and the beginning."[10]

If we lose contact with the priority of the apostolic witness, we will also lose contact with the end. The apostolic witness is to be embodied in every local, particular manifestation of the church, and that makes it universal, one, and holy.[11] Apostolicity and the other two marks are inseparable from "holiness." Congar notes, "The Church's oneness is holy. It is different from the phenomenon described by sociologists and is to be found at the level of faith. The Church's apostolicity is also holy. It is the continuity of a mission and a communion which begin in God. Finally, the catholicity of the Church is holy and different from for example, a multi-national or world-wide expansion."[12] Just to have a global corporation is insufficient. We already have many of them. Nor is it adequate to have a federation of autonomous bodies—we already have that, it is called the "United Nations." The purpose of the church, its ineluctable witness, requires a global *communion* where each does not live individualistically like an "idiot," but in common. What is held in common is what Wesley identified—doctrine, worship, life. But all of this is for the purpose of a social embodiment of the life of beatitude. A "bare" orthodoxy or common liturgy is insufficient without its fruit in the common life of beatitude, the life of holiness. This brings us back to Wesley. For the "holiness" of the church is its participation in Christ's work through the Holy Spirit. For Wesley, the beatitudes constitute that work. For what are they but the righteousness exhibited in Christ's own work? His righteousness is

---

10. Ibid., 39.
11. Ibid., 26–27.
12. Ibid., 52.

to become our righteousness, the righteousness of his body, the church, through its application to us by the Holy Spirit. Communion without beatitude is not communion; it is form without substance.

The Anglican Mission

Four years ago, while teaching at Garrett Evangelical Theological Seminary on the campus of Northwestern University, one of my students came to me and mentioned that he was part of a new church plant that intended to start a ministry at Northwestern. He asked if I would consider being the faculty sponsor. When Mike Niebauer, the catechist for this new ministry, explained the vision for it, I was attracted because its primary purpose was to do evangelism not as a program, but through a common way of life. Mike was a graduate of Northwestern and he thought Christians on NU's campus had been too influenced by a kind of evangelicalism that was solitary and individual. It lacked community and connection with the classical Christian tradition, both in doctrine and worship. He wanted to start a community that would remedy this. I explained to him how Wesley's general rules functioned, and we did two things. First, we began a Sunday worship service in the Anglican tradition where we fulfilled the third general rule by providing for both NU students and Garrett seminarians a weekly Eucharist where we could also confess our common faith in the Nicene Creed, something that has disappeared in Methodist churches. We requested and were originally granted the use of Garrett's chapel for this service, although we were eventually asked to leave. Second, we formed a number of small groups that met regularly in order to pursue holiness by using the Methodist General Rules. We had NU undergrads and Garrett seminarians praying together in these discipleship groups for two years. I found this to be an exciting and hopeful development where the vision of Wesley and its rightful place in the Anglican Communion were coming together. We were, and are, something of a hybrid identity—not trying to avoid the proper role of the hierarchical offices in the church, but more concerned for the life of holiness embodied in the local faith community.

After two years of working with the Church of the Redeemer at Northwestern, for reasons that still mystify me, we were asked to leave Garrett's campus. By that time we were an officially recognized ministry at Northwestern University, so the ministry continued on NU's campus.

I have since left Garrett, but Mike carried on the vision and they still graciously allow me to preach when I can. He, along with others, continues the vision of catechists starting small, local communities bound by a common life of doctrine, worship, and the pursuit of holiness. I still find this resonant with Wesley's vision and wonder if in the future the Spirit might lead us to a renewed communion between Wesleyans and Anglicans.[13] Church of Redeemer at NU continues with small discipleship groups. They still provide a weekly Anglican Eucharist service, but no longer with any official cooperation from the Methodist seminary. They are raising up leaders who will start similar ministries at other Midwest universities.

Conclusion

Let me offer some concluding comments as an outsider—as a Methodist who longs for a visible global communion—on the present crisis besetting Anglicanism. I must confess that as a Methodist who had worked primarily in Catholic settings, I knew little about the crisis in the Anglican Communion when I consented to be the faculty sponsor for Church of Redeemer at Northwestern. I know a bit more about it now and I would be pleased that, if by God's grace, the crisis among Anglicans could result in bringing us back in to that communion. We Methodists were a movement that accidentally became a church, and we do not do church well. We need the order, discipline, and common liturgy of the Anglican Communion, just as it could benefit from our emphasis on holiness. Somehow, in opposition to Wesley, we thought we could have the substance of holiness without the form of the general rules, the creeds, and a common liturgy. That has not worked well. However, I think we could also contribute our charism to the Anglican Communion. The purpose of the order of the church is not an end it itself but a means to embody Christ's life.

It does not come as a surprise to me that the Church of England and The Episcopal Church in the United States experienced an acute crisis at the end of Christendom, one that has struck and will strike most of Protestantism, but surely there is a reason that it struck this church so forcibly. Turning to Wesley might help us understand why.

---

13. I'm encouraged that Mike's band is called "John Wesley's Band," which can be found online: http://www.myspace.com/johnwesleysband.

John Wesley proclaimed that the "mystery of iniquity" arose in the Church when Christians were no longer willing to claim that they were "of one heart and mind" and no one's possessions were his or her own. For him, the "lasting wound" to the Church was when Constantine "called himself a Christian, and poured in a flood of riches, honours, and power upon the Christians, more especially upon the clergy."[14] This individuated the Church and made it more committed to acting like the nations of the world rather than being "for the healing of the nations."[15] Is this not in large part the crisis before us? It is the crisis of "Constantinianism," which does not refer only to the events in the fourth century. (I am well aware that Justinian in the sixth century was much more Constantinian than Constantine.) It refers to the Casearopapism in which throne and altar are brought together into a unity such that the church primarily serves the interests of the ruling authorities. Perhaps it is my Methodist background or the fact that I work in a Catholic setting, but it seems to me that insofar as the unity of the Anglican Communion is defined by the Archbishop of Canterbury—given how he is appointed—this lingering problem of "Caesaropapism," or at least "investiture," remains. This is not because I have any animus toward the Archbishop—in fact I am a huge fan of the theology of the present holder—but because I think identifying the office of unity through a single, nationalist identity (appointed by the Queen and Prime Minister) continues the improper individuation of a catholic communion.

Of course, the problem is not just the Church of England—another version of "Constantinianism" and/or investiture can be found in TEC. Note the language by which the "Chicago Consultation" recently challenged the proposed Anglican covenant:

> The Episcopal Church was founded shortly after the American Revolution. In keeping with that democratic tradition, the Church's constitution and canons and its historical polity provide us with both the strength and stability of the General Convention's governing and legislative processes as well as the local ability for dioceses to discern and elect the bishops who can best serve them and make other decisions about their common life. We believe that these canons have served us well, are essential to the Church's continued

---

14. "Mystery of Iniquity," II.463.
15. Ibid., II.466.

> health and bind together the strongest elements of our common spiritual heritage and tradition of democracy.

The specifics of the American national polity provide the basis for the ecclesial polity in opposition to the catholicity of the Church. Once again, the Church is improperly individuated. Communion cannot take place when our national traditions, be they British, American, Canadian, or African, take precedence over what we hold in common.

I recognize that this is an easy accusation to make, but more difficult to defend, and yet more difficult to remedy. Nonetheless, I find wisdom in Wesley's diagnosis. As long as any part of the body refuses to hold in common our possessions, including our sacred possessions, will we not continue to experience our lingering wounds?

SIX

Apostolic Ministry Revisited

George Sumner

What does the Great Tradition have to say about community? At its best, precious little! If you were to take the multiple volumes of the *Summa Theologiae* of Thomas Aquinas, and you were to search them diligently for the section dealing with ecclesiology, the doctrine of the church, you would find, well, nothing. Sections on bishops, on martyrdom, on doctrine, on sacraments, on schism, but nothing on the Christian community *per se*. And why? Because fish do not reflect on water—they swim in it. Now it is not quite true that the tradition has nothing to say on the doctrine of the church, but most of what it does have is not coincidentally related to moments of rupture and crisis—Cyprian on what to do with apostates, Cusanus on what to do as a result of having three popes, Luther on what to do when people start selling forgiveness.

It is on this score that we may profitably compare the word "community" to the closely related word "tradition." Whether you are a revisionist or a traditionalist, worrying about the word means that the thing itself has broken down. Tradition, like the fish's water, is what you do not see when it is all in good working order. (Something similar may be said of method in systematics, and hermeneutics in Bible, if we turn our attention to theology, but that is a story for another day.) Poignant example that he is for those of us who are fathers, Reb Tevye booms forth, "Tradition, the papa!" as the mores change progressively for each of his daughters, and his cry of assertion means that the thing itself has been called into question.

Let me offer another example closer to home. More often than not, when the Wycliffe student council is asked for a topic for the fall retreat, one that will help the incoming seminarians, the theme comes back "community." They hope their new *confreres*, soon to lead busy lives on the fly, will have an experience of being bonded, of sharing a set of hopes and fears. From praise band to trash-talking volleyball to long conversations over forgettable camp food, they often do have such an experience. But community is really found, more imperceptibly, in the slow grind of the weekly round, praying, thinking, struggling, in a common place, with a common set of doctrinal commitments, and a shared faculty to be frustrated with! The call for community declares its endangered status, and its discovery is not something we confect, but something we find to be a given of a common life.

What are the deep-structural theological realities beneath the question of community in the Scriptures? First is the fact of God's calling of a people, Israel, of which identity we partake in Christ. We are called into a people whose identity is a given, prior to and outside of ourselves. This givenness is entailed in what we mean by "grace." This is a central point of the Old Testament. We cannot construct or confect our identity any more than we decide on a Savior. Nor is this identity an individual possession. We must hasten to add, secondly, that the individual decision of faith is vital in the New Testament. That theme opens on to the great questions about divine and human will in the Great Tradition of theology, since our decision is overshadowed by God's sovereign will. In its light alone we come to understand what human freedom, repaired and healed, really is—such was Augustine's great illumination of the Pauline truth. To summarize, communal identity is neither the result of human will, nor does it occlude the individual, whose tragedy, dignity, and hope we see in the light of grace. So individual and community have their own meanings in the New Testament determined by grace. The New Testament would put the question before us on its own terms.

But all this is in strong contrast with what modernity means by "community" and "individual"—a different grammar is at work. As contemporary Christians, we live in the zone between the two, where decoding the secular is a missionary imperative. The point is a simple one to state but a hard one to overcome, since we are talking about how we see ourselves, and the world, in a basic way.

At one level, as we have said, the tradition says little about ecclesiology because it presumes the encompassing reality of the church. But as time goes on, much of it grows out of ecclesial division, for community is problematic in the Great Tradition itself. The divisions of the church lead to polemics toward one another. To be sure, in the ecumenical work of the modern era we have rediscovered the shared commitments, the common allegiance to Mere Christianity, which lies beneath these divisions. But differences in ecclesial traditions are not meaningless, nor can they be overlooked. As to community, the pot in which we receive the Gospel treasure is cracked and even at the dawn of the modern era required some kind of repair.

Of course things only get worse in the modern era, and the confusion over community becomes pervasive in a new way. Peter Berger, for example, in his *The Heretical Imperative*, argues that "we are all heretics" now.[1] He refers here to the meaning of the Greek word (*hairetikos*), literally "choice." In the modern world, we all choose for ourselves what we shall believe (even if our choice should be conservative Anglicanism), and we imagine this choosing to be what constitutes ourselves as individuals. Self and so world are constructed from within. The same observation pervades the work of the contemporary Canadian Catholic philosopher Charles Taylor. The central argument of the book *Sources of Self* has to do with the pressure felt by individual selves to solve their own problems.

It is not only secular people, then, who must make decisions east of Eden in a church of rupture and competition. I have come to believe, but in which corner of the church, or indeed of Anglicanism, should I serve? Aidan Kavanagh, the noted liturgical theologian, was driven around the bend by divinity students who would say, "I figured out my ministry, now I need a church in which to practice it," as if the cart could pull the ox. But Kavanagh notwithstanding, this is a real question for devout members of our student body. And to make matters even more perplexing, there is a pervasive sense in our time that spirituality, including orthodox Christian spirituality, is more appealing than structures of the church, which involve the depressingly institutional. But the Great Tradition, which knows

---

1. Peter Berger, *The Heretical Imperative* (New York: Doubleday, 1979).

a great deal about spirituality, knows nothing of a Christianity that is separate from the concrete realities of the church, its doctrine, its forms of authority, its means of organization, etc. (It may be noted that the first reference to "spirituality" is in Shakespeare, where it is contrasted to secularity and refers to bishops, synods, authority, etc.)

Community is a gift and, as such, a given, but it is twice broken, once within the tradition and once again and more deeply, outside of it in modernity. Where, in response, are we to begin? The classical passage for our consideration is Acts 2:

> They were persistent in the teaching of the apostles, and in the common life, in the breaking of the bread and in the prayers . . . many signs and wonders occurred through the apostles. All the believers were together, and had all things in common. And they sold all their possessions and goods, and divided them up as any had need. They were consistently together in the Temple, and at home breaking bread and took their nourishment with joy and generosity of heart, praising God and having favor with all people. And the Lord added those being saved to the same every day. (Acts 2:43, 45–47)

Everything about the apostles is predicated on what God has done, particularly in the resurrection and ascension that set the stage for Acts, and now on what God is at work doing in the community. Everything is also predicated on what time it is, the time of repentance, of calling the Gentiles, of expectation of the summation of all things—"conversion," "baptism," and "Spirit" all bring an eschatological thought to mind.

So it is the category of the "apostle" that is the crucial one in thinking about community in the Great Tradition. Community gathered around the apostle, and true community maintains the apostolic. To be sure it is only one of the marks of the church, but the others may be understood in relation to it—unity is the congealing around the apostle, holiness is life maintained in that way, and catholicity the worldwide reach of such communities throughout the world. It can be noted at this point that the argument over community in an earlier, less dissipated, generation of the Anglican Church, was precisely over the nature of the apostolic. The arguments of the Anglo-Catholics, locating the apostolic in the office of the bishop *per se*, and of the evangelicals, locating the apostolic in the inherited teaching of which the bishop is a sign and guardian, have a distant innocence to contemporary ears, but at least they point to a key category around which reflection on community will circle.

Secondly, we observe that the Acts 2 passage intertwines various dimensions of *to koinon*, that which they hold in common, community, communion: the teaching they receive, their time together, their goods, their faithfulness as children of Israel, the table of the Lord, their praise. It is in light of this passage that we are in position to consider the expression *communio in sacris*, which is usually taken to mean ecumenical sharing in the form of shared sacramental life. But one can extend the sense of "communion in the sacred" to sharing in holy things in a wider sense— sacramentally holy acts, the holy words of Scripture, the holy life. Acts 2 is often understood as presenting to us an ideal picture of such communion, a kind of maximalist account of what Christians in communion would share. Though we may not wish to go this far, surely the "holy things" should include all the dimensions we have listed.

By contrast we might consider all the minimalist accounts of what community is, with which the contemporary Anglican scene is littered. We might say that one feature of concepts of the church in our time is that they tend to be one-dimensional. Into the inherited situation of division one person finds community in an experience of closeness or being together. Another finds it in the mere fact of saying the liturgy together, and receiving communion as one, what we called the "orthopraxy" approach. Others would detour around conflict with a sheer appeal to mission— "Leave all that aside, and let's together pursue what God is doing more widely." Others chime in and find some ethical dimension or other as itself constitutive—for example, pacifism, or solidarity in social justice, etc. We as conservatives would insist that the place of doctrinal definition cannot be lost, though it will not suffice alone. Acts 2 reminds us that thinning-out type definitions will not do—but where then should we turn?

In 1987, I was a priest on a reservation in the Southwest. It was the year of the new-age harmonic convergence. The planets were in alignment. Hippies from all over North America, awakened like so many Rip Van Winkles, passed through on their way to Sedona, a place of interest due to its whorl geological formations, thought to soon be transformed into space ships. One latter day P. T. Barnum sold seats on the ship for $100, then sold standing-room-only for $150. Only in America! Well you will be relieved to learn that I am not advocating harmonic convergence, but I am advocating something I would call "apostolic convergence." By this I mean the gracious ability, in the twofold quandary I have described, to reach beyond ourselves, to rediscover our commonality in the Gospel, to allow the apostolic to overcome centrifugal forces, and in so doing to give real substance to the idea of an embodiment of the Gospel, in key moments of Church history. Community presents itself as the possibility of such an act, as in each historical moment we look for such an apostolic convergence. So with most of the time that remains to me I want to describe three such moments, each with an Anglican angle, each with a lesson to teach us.

The first example of a moment of apostolic convergence which I would offer to you is the Synod of Whitby, presided over in the year 664 in Northumbria by the Abbess St. Hilda in her convent. You will recall that the presenting issues were the date for the celebration of Easter and the shape of tonsure required of a monk, which you would not think were, in the jargon of our day, "core doctrine" at all. Yet these can come to epitomize two kinds of Christianity, the Roman and the Celtic. (All this has a special kind of appropriateness in our time given the appeal of the Celtic, and the appeals made to it as a source of an alternative model for Anglican polity.) The friction between these two forms of the Nicene faith were resolved successfully at the Synod. We might point to the authority of the king, patron, and presider at the gathering, though this alone is too simple. If we consider the debate, it offered competing precedents from the apostolic tradition, the Roman appeal to Peter finally winning the day. But all agreed that such a debate, with such a criterion, would be required, and in so agreeing they already proved to have more in common than separately. Both sides looked to the sanctity of their outstanding leaders in a manner which tempered their contest, in particular the example of St. Hilda herself. The synod took cognizance of the wider church, where the Roman observance had come to prevail. Finally the synod took place in the aftermath of a plague, with the threat of the Picts, Britons, and Angles, and so the common challenge of its devastation placed everyone in a changed circumstance. There was a sufficient fund of shared sense of the apostolic tradition in its fuller sense, and a shared sense of missionary urgency, to allow them to overcome their competing senses of the precise form of the apostolic. (And it should be added the Celtic strain was never lost altogether, but in a sense subordinated in English Christianity.) In this case conflicting churches could move toward unity as they reached back for apostolic precedents, outward in relation to contemporary crisis, and toward one another by the common perception of an apostolic form of life.

The second example of apostolic convergence relates directly to the life of one of the greatest missionary and mission theologians of our own era, Lesslie Newbigin. His life spanned most of the great missionary rallying cries of our time—he was party to the formation of the "mission of God" trend of thought in the 1950s, and its cousin, the Trinitarian theology of mission. He reacted against its offspring, the secular city idea. And he is the father of the idea of mission to the West in light of a post-Christendom, post-Enlightenment epistemology. But even before he espoused all of these ideas, he was intimately involved in one of the great ecumenical movements of the latter half of the twentieth century: the creation of the Church of South India. The reunion was the fruit of a half century of missionary cooperation among Protestants which fed directly into the ecumenical movement. To put it succinctly, the differences between Presbyterian and Anglican fade in contrast to a resurgent neo-Hinduism in a land in which Christians are but a couple of percentage points of the population. In other words, a horizon of sharp cultural difference, and of the missionary imperative it brings, made a material difference. (As an aside, it is worth noting some of the social circumstances. Those successful in joining together shared a common background in nineteenth-century transdenominational evangelistic groups—YMCA being prominent. They wrote for the same Christian journals, went to the same Christian schools, and attended the same renewal conferences. Furthermore, for all its problems, episcopacy came to be seen positively as a bulwark against caste.)

As with other reunion schemes in the earlier twentieth century, the sticky wicket was that very episcopate, and more particularly, how those two senses of the apostolic, centered either on the person or on the teaching, relate one to another. The great step forward was to think about moving toward regularizing relations over time—to set the whole challenge in relation to a reconciled future. So, with the CSI, ministries were recognized in the present and unconditionally, but with the understanding that future ordinations would include bishops in apostolic succession (this was borrowed in the talks between Anglicans and Lutherans in North America). The oneness we share in Christ was both recognized and the church moved toward a goal, a *telos*. This was a richer sense of the prize of the upward call in Christ Jesus than had earlier been employed (and it has been used since among Anglicans in North America). We might summarize the matter this way: convergence was based on the real commonality of apostolic life, and on the deeper meaning of the apostolic in relation to the mission to declare the resurrection, to which the office, the structure, would catch up. Christians of different and related traditions could see themselves as one in Christ based on Word and sacrament in the broad sense, and were determined to move toward that reality in the concrete realities of their life. This convergence as discipline and act is surely consistent with what we mean by community in the Great Tradition.

At one level, then, community is simply fellowship Christians have in their confession of Jesus. It is an act of submission to an identity given before us and hence between us. But it is also an act of convergence in critical historical circumstances in which we find anew the unity between us as we reach back to the apostles, outward and ahead in relation to the mission to evangelize the Gentiles in this the last times, all seen more brightly against the background of the non-Christian world.

At this point we can expand our reflection and note that "apostolic convergence" may be not only a description of the dimensions of some historical *rapprochement*, but also a template for the retrieval in general of the apostolic, whether in individuals or groups. One could even find in these dimensions a way of presenting the features usually attributed to Anglican ecclesiology, including bishops, synods, and attention to context.

What common features may be identified in these two examples of what I have called, in two very different ecumenical conundra, apostolic enactment? What are the conditions for the possibility of a shared ecclesial life with new vitality? In both Northumbria and Madras we may identify (at least) four dimensions of the situation in which a new and yet faithful apostolic framework was found. First of all, and most importantly, different and yet related Christians were able to reach backward behind their separations in order to move forward. They could appeal backward to the shared apostolic tradition. In each case this enabled them to suffuse the apostolic form, namely the episcopate, representing as it does Christian leadership as a whole, with apostolic content. The two are only explicable together. The church after all is only the church, and so only able to be the old holy catholic and apostolic church, as it hears the Gospel which lends definition to all those adjectives.

Secondly, we may say that in both cases the stark realization of a demandingly alien and pagan environment came home to the church. It somehow saw that it could not afford to carry the baggage of old divisions. (This was overcome not by making light of them, but by thinking and praying past them.) In the case of Bede's Northumbria, both Celtic and Latin Christians were at risk in the face of the invading and bellicose Saxon.[2] In the case of the Church of South India, the vast difference between traditional Christian faith of any vein and their Hindu neighbors made the differences between Methodist, Presbyterian, and Anglican fade into lesser significance. They received the grace of having the luxury of division removed. Thirdly, both churches were to their very bones evangelistic communities. They were able to see the apostolic inheritance which was to be proclaimed, and the unbelieving neighbor as the one to whom they must proclaim. The structure of the church was not dissolved into a mere means for mission, but it could be rethought in relation to it. (In fact, I would suggest that the truly missional church has exactly these four features.) Fourthly, we find in both examples appeal not only to the form and content of the apostolic, but to its process as well, namely the conciliar. (This feature has been brought to prominence recently in theological circles by my friend and colleague, Ephraim Radner.) Shared inheritance, shared risk, shared great commission led to a sharing of the councils of the church. This was not an easy process in either case—in the first the Celts felt hard done by, in the second the Anglo-Catholics had objections of conscience that nearly scuttled the plan. But in both cases these four features of apostolic enactment—form and content, the pagan neighbor, mission, and the conciliar—concretely changed the way that the church involved understood themselves.

Of course the third example I would give to you is harder, since it is still unfolding. I speak to you as one who has remained within the Anglican Church of Canada to be part of those who witness to the Gospel as Scripture presents it, in the hope of renewal so that the future might present a more orthodox Anglican face. This is of course not the answer that all Anglicans in North America have offered to the crisis in which we find ourselves. But what we all share is an appeal in some way or other to the apostolic inheritance, to our goodly heritage as we find it reaching back to our past or out to our far-flung global neighbors. So all of us struggle to be apostolic in both form and content. In short I am arguing that we all need to see ourselves, together, in a manner analogous to our ancestors in Northumbria and Madras. Let us then measure ourselves against the other three factors—we need to see in our predicament but

2. The best source is of course Bede himself in *Ecclesiastical History of the English People* (London: Penguin, 1990) 243–47.

one symptom of the ravages of modernity, its individualism and relativism, on Christianity as a whole. That is the pagan culture of which we all share. The enemy is within and well as without, and against such an enemy traditional Christians need a renewed commitment to solidarity. In the face of this opponent (not just this or that bishop or theologian or blogger), we need to think of ourselves as a disciplined minority community whose primary task is missionary. This is extremely difficult in circumstances which are increasingly pressured by liberal leadership. But we must do it regardless, for the evangelistic appeal of the Canterbury Trail, of Christianity in an evangelically Anglican mode, continues. Finally we need to be in council together, with one another, with Anglicans who support us, with Anglicans who do not. This conciliar life is quite simply an apostolic Christian practice, a dimension of apostolicity. As such it can have consequences quite beyond our own calculations of utility or futility, by the grace of the Holy Spirit.

Apostolic convergence: what does this say to the intersection of traditional and emergent? Insofar as we all struggle as modern Christians, we are all already brothers and sisters. We all face our own willfulness, even in our justifiable acts of reclaiming. I am also noting, more optimistically, that there are mainstays of ecclesiology, emerging from the Gospel, which in fact we all would acknowledge when they are articulated: the apostolic in form and content, the neighbor, the Great Commission, Christians taking counsel. With this recognition, we must submit ourselves to the Gospel represented concretely by these. I suspect in each mainstay the test is obedience in the face of resistance over time. So the concomitant virtue with apostolic convergence is endurance. We are not all monks, but we all need to hear in our time the call to stability.

From the Anglican side, a resurgent theology of the sacraments as evangelical practice will be entailed in apostolic convergence. The Eucharist is the enjoyment of Christ's presence over time; in baptism Christians are formed toward and from their new identity. In proclaiming forgiveness we hear that God's grace continues to work in a broken church. From the side of the emergent, the newcomer, the fellow-traveler, we are recalled to our own missionary history, and we see our ancestors afresh as heroes of the faith. We are reminded that the practices of the church need to be tested for Gospel content.

The treasure is indeed in a contingent, broken, alienated clay pot. So we are called to converge, brothers and sisters, on this gracious rediscovery, of the *ecclesia* in its gracious and given fragility.

I have cited Lesslie Newbigin and the CSI's birth. Let me close with a quotation from the opening pages of his *South India Diary*:

> As the cathedral bell strikes eight, the service of inauguration opens and the long procession representing the three uniting Churches moves up the centre aisle of the cathedral. We join in prayer and then listen to the reading of the great High Priestly prayer in the power of which alone all these long years of wrestling with our divisions have been possible. Then on our knees we confess afresh that our unity, holiness, truth are in him alone and not in us . . . . A great peal from the organ breaks in upon the words and in a moment four thousand voices burst into the Te Deum in one tremendous shout of praise. All the long-frustrated desires of these painful years have burst through the dam . . . with God all things are possible . . . . What has been done? Not, if we speak strictly, the inauguration of a "church." There can be but one Church. What has been done is that something which hid the true character of the Church has been repented of, and a very small step has been taken toward putting it away. Even that little step could not have been taken without the tremendous and ceaseless constraint of God's Word and Spirit. Now there is a sense of joy and release. God save us from settling down again.[3]

---

3. Lesslie Newbigin, *A South India Diary* (London: SCM, 1951) 12.

SEVEN

Emerging Church: A Victorian Prequel

Dominic Erdozain

The strangest thing about being a historian is that you gain a surer grasp of times and places you can never visit than your own. This can put you out of touch with the world around you, but it occasionally provides insights that are transformative. I will never forget sitting in the natural history library in Oxford, reading a book by Robert Young called *Darwin's Metaphor: Nature's Place in Victorian Culture* (1985). It was my first exposure to the new, cultural history of science, and the revelations of Darwin's debts to his cultural milieu were stunning. It shattered the comforting, binary oppositions on which my thoughts had rested, and I had a strange urge to stand up and inform the quietly industrious scientists present of the relativities of their craft. Darwin had been earthed in the chaotic authenticity of his times, and rather than using science to explain history, Young was using history to explain science. Learning, we are told, relies on judicious bursts of "cognitive dissonance," and here was dissonance of an exhilarating kind. Everything was up for negotiation. Darwin was no visitor to his culture: he was part of it.

It was one thing to start thinking about science in this way. But could Christianity bend to the winds of cultural change and still be

Christianity? Could the mystical chain of faith and confession be seen not just to inhabit history but to be forged and remade by it? That was the next cognitive "leap" and the idea behind this paper. The past is rich in resources for the church, and one of the riches is the example of how faithful Christians have "reformed, that they may preserve": reinventing the modes of Christian expression in order to restore its essence. The clearest and, to my mind, most startling example was the evangelical appropriation of the Enlightenment. Brought up to think of Descartes' *cogito ergo sum* as a kind of second "Fall" for Western humanity, I was surprised to read that Evangelicalism had anything to do with this surge of humanistic confidence. Having paced up and down wondering whether this is simply the nature of academia to posit theories that everyone knows to be untrue, it eventually clicked: the age of revival and mission would not have happened without a breaking of the communal ethic of pre-modern culture. This did not mean that evangelicals were individualists, but it did mean that they had to step away from the inherited structures of the faith before they could engage their culture. They were the pioneers of emerging church. The challenges that we are inclined to interpret under the rubric of "postmodernity"—fragmentation and alienation, vertigo-inducing epistemologies—were *eighteenth-century* problems, and it is ironic that while emergent theologies pull away from the systems and certainties of a mature evangelicalism, they reprise the drama and impatience of the movement's youth. Evangelicalism, with its formulae, pragmatism, and set-piece moralism, may now represent "the problem" for many who would recover the suppleness of New Testament mission: the shrewd candor of Paul on the Areopagus. But this is to forget the movement's brave legacy of cultural synthesis—what David Hempton has termed a tradition of "inspired innovation based on biblical ideas."[1] And if evangelicalism ultimately became too cozy with some of the impulses of modernity, this is no danger to which emerging churches are immune: the snares of the modern were subtle, incidental, and incremental rather than overt or intrinsic. If, as I will argue, evangelicalism was quietly disabled by a permanent itch for relevance, emerging churches might heed the warning.

Innovation, then, has a long history. We are told that, after seventeen centuries, the era of "Christendom" is finally drawing to a close and

---

1. David Hempton, *Methodism and Politics in British Society 1750–1850* (London: Hutchinson, 1984) 29.

"everything must change."² The truth is that "Christendom," that ancient and contested alliance between Christ and Caesar, was an unworkable concept by the early eighteenth century. The "Godly Commonwealth" of New England, and the British "confessional state," were each, in their way, creaking under the pressures of dissent and divergence. Roger Williams, founder of Providence, Rhode Island, argued as much in his searing text, *The Bloody Tenet of Persecution for Cause of Conscience* (1644), but it took a great deal more bloodshed before toleration became a reality. The eighteenth century saw the beginnings of religious liberty, but the state churches lived on, united in disdain for religious "enthusiasm." Yoked to secular power and increasingly dry in theology, they were custodial rather than pastoral in tone. Christianity was a gatekeeper for a hierarchical and often oppressive society, and both intellectuals and common people started to drift away—psychologically if not physically.

There have been valiant attempts to relieve the eighteenth-century Church of England of its reputation for complacency, corruption, and pastoral neglect, but the strongest argument has been that, given the society in which it operated, sins of elitism and nepotism were to be expected. This is what is known as "going native" with your subject matter. Historians have swooned over poetic accounts of life in the parishes, celebrating the way in which the Prayer Book was endeared to English hearts by its "melodic Cranmerian prose." "People with no education at all knew large portions of it by heart simply by hearing it so often," writes one historian.³ The picture is akin to Samuel Palmer's celebrated *Coming from Evening Church* (1830) in which a vicar leads his flock into a gorgeous, moonlit landscape. It was a beautiful, and imagined, world.

Official ecclesiology remained Richard Hooker's sixteenth-century notion that, "There is not any man of the *Church of England*, but the same man is also a member of the *Commonwealth*; nor any man a member of the *Commonwealth* which is not also of the *Church of England*."⁴ The reality was otherwise, as those who revived this organic rhetoric knew well. John Walsh has written of "the sense of interior decay that afflicted

---

2. See Stuart Murray, *Church after Christendom* (London: Paternoster, 2005); Brian McLaren, *Everything Must Change: Jesus, Global Crises, and a Revolution of Hope* (Nashville: Thomas Nelson, 2008).

3. Antony Waterman, quoted in Stewart Jay Brown, *The National Churches of England, Ireland, and Scotland, 1801–1846* (Oxford: Oxford University Press, 2001) 6.

4. Richard Hooker, quoted in Brown, *Churches*, 7.

much of Protestantism" in the eighteenth century,[5] and one study of rural religion in England was so struck by the weakness of Christianity at the popular level, it called for a revolution of historical understanding: "The 'Ptolemaic' theory of popular religion—with Christianity at its centre and paganism at the fringes—will need to undergo a 'Copernican revolution.'" The influence of Christian ideas among the rural poor was, at best, superficial and, at worst, non-existent. "Paganism was dominant, and Christianity, recessive in popular religion," it was concluded.[6] Defenders of the eighteenth-century Church have either ignored the question of popular piety, or fallen into the sociological error of regarding magic and religion as part of the same, pre-modern religiosity, and not enquiring into content. I agree with David Martin in seeing the religious boom that followed the spiritual depression as a process of *"re-Christianization"*—a combative reaction to "the [secularizing] inroads made over the eighteenth century."[7] It would not have occurred without a revolution in Christian communication and organization. Charles Wesley's hymns, combining the raptures of personal faith with the exuberance of English folk melodies, were the symbol of a movement that was almost parasitic in its debts to contemporary culture.

Paradoxically, the first major debt was philosophical. The contagious idea that salvation could be known with almost physical exactitude owed much to John Locke. John Wesley and Jonathan Edwards used Locke's "sensationalist epistemology" to reconceive conversion with unprecedented clarity. The message they took from Locke was that ideas only register meaningfully when appropriated personally. Religious concepts, like any other, have to be sensed to be believed. Second-hand authorities are suspect because they do the thinking for you and deprive you of the thrilling certainty on which true knowledge depends. Modernity, in a sense, starts here. And Wesley's urgent aspiration, "I want that faith which none can have without knowing that he hath it," was its Christian

---

5. John Walsh, "'Methodism' and the Origins of English-speaking Evangelicalism," In *Evangelicalism: Comparative Studies of Popular Protestantism in North America, the British Isles and Beyond, 1700–1990*, Religion in America series (Oxford: Oxford University Press, 1994) 20.

6. James Obelkevich, *Religion and Rural Society, South Lindsey, 1825–1875* (Oxford: Clarendon, 1976) 306–9.

7. David Martin, *On Secularization: Towards a Revised General Theory* (Aldershot, UK: Ashgate, 2005) 124.

expression.[8] We worry now about the danger of *exalting* experience, but in the eighteenth century, experiential certainty was a lifeline. Walsh referred to the "psychic strain" felt by many believers in this period, schooled in the wearying disciplines of "holy living." "There was a certain joylessness in the call to a regime of unrelenting worship, closet devotion, introspection, and asceticism," he wrote. The Calvinist suspicion of "assurance" was, in the words of a London Dissenter explaining his conversion to Methodism, "like a general's commanding his soldiers to fight on towards taking . . . a city and at the same time telling them they must never expect to take it."[9] There is little doubt that Enlightenment empiricism, with its startling confidence in personal experience, was one of the levers that burst the psychic dam. The forces may have been of the old Sea of Faith; the mechanisms that unleashed them were distinctly modern.

The clearest example is Jonathan Edwards, who did more than anyone to build intellectual structures for the revival on both sides of the Atlantic.[10] The Christianity of his youth had lurched emphatically toward the disciplinary and cognitive side of the faith. The result was a stern and precarious spirituality that seemed strangely out of step with the New Testament. Flashes of emotion were routinely repressed. Divine sovereignty was emphasized to the point of crushing human initiative. Piety was a journey mapped out in meticulous detail by the "giants" of Puritan divinity. Church membership was confined to those who had completed each separate "step" of regeneration. What John Wesley termed "High Church Pelagianism" had a new world imitator.[11] The turning point for Edwards was seeing "some hundreds of townspeople" anxiously "seeking grace" after a Sunday service. Yet "only thirteen" met his father's strict criteria and were allowed to join the church "in an estate of full communion." The young Edwards was mystified and privately "resolved never to leave searching till I have satisfyingly found out the very bottom and foundation, the real reason, why they used to be converted in those steps." He determined (after an argument with his father) to increase his knowledge of Scripture—"the one authority that could trump Puritan

---

8. D. W. Bebbington, *Evangelicalism in Modern Britain: A History from the 1730's to the 1980's* (London: Unwin Hyman, 1989) 49. I am greatly indebted to this seminal text in the sections that follow.

9. Walsh, "Methodism," 26, 30.

10. Bebbington, *Evangelicalism*, 65.

11. Walsh, "Methodism," 28.

divines." The result was a framework for nurturing, rather than suppressing, spiritual affections, which would serve "to redirect the thought of Christendom."[12]

The key text was the *Treatise on Religious Affections* (1746), which used Lockean psychology to establish the certainty of the conversion process. Edwards wrote of a "new sensation or perception in the mind" wrought by God in conversion. "There is," he wrote, "what some metaphysicians call a new simple idea."[13] Spiritual sensation or "holy affections" passed from suspicion to acceptance, and the effects were explosive. Marsden talks about the redirection of Christendom, but Mark Noll suggests that the new emphasis on personal covenant was sufficient to destroy the corporate unities of New England Puritanism.[14] The sacred canopy fractured, and the life beneath flourished. Edwards, for his own part, could not resist organic imagery:

> Grace in many persons, through this ignorance of their state, and their looking on themselves still as the objects of God's displeasure, has been like the trees in winter, or like seed in the spring suppressed under a hard clod of earth . . . . But when they have been better instructed, and so brought to allow of *hope*, this has awakened the gracious disposition of their hearts into life and vigour as the warm beams of the sun in spring have quickened the seeds and productions of the earth.[15]

The power of this image is the harmony between human initiative—"better instruct[ion]"—and the release of divine energy—"the warm beams of the sun." Grace is of God, but God is neither distant nor inscrutable. Locke did not "make" Edwards, any more than Thomas Malthus "made" Darwin, but there was a critical exchange, a seminal moment, and people who never got near the technicalities of Enlightenment philosophy shared the mood of release. Wesley, who hid his intellectual debts and cultivated the image of the *homo unius libri*—a man of the one Book—exuded the spirit of confidence and clarity. "I design plain truth

---

12. In the words of George M. Marsden, in *Jonathan Edwards: A Life* (New Haven: Yale University Press, 2003) 58.

13. Jonathan Edwards, *A Treatise Concerning Religious Affections, in Three Parts* (J. Crissy, 1821) 137.

14. Mark A. Noll, *America's God: From Jonathan Edwards to Abraham Lincoln* (Oxford: Oxford University Press, 2002) 39ff.

15. Quoted in Bebbington, *Evangelicalism*, 47.

for plain people," he wrote; and his hymnbook was subtitled, "A little body of practical and experimental divinity." Then there was George Whitefield, whose flamboyant, open-air preaching crystallized the iconoclasm of the revival—what Noll has termed its "antitraditionalism":

> Whitefield's preaching broke traditional rules; it called for direct, immediate response; it encouraged the laity to perform Christian services that were the historical preserve of the clergy. Whitefield and his imitators did not read their sermons like most of the colonies' settled ministers of the early eighteenth century but declaimed them extemporaneously in order to maximize their power. Whitefield's speech drove home the lesson that it was not formal education or a prestigious role in the community that ultimately mattered but *the choice of an individual for or against God*. Whitefield was the colonies' most visible symbol of changing conceptions of hierarchy; he represented a new confidence in the religious powers of the people and a sharp, if implicit, rebuke to the authority of tradition.[16]

Whitefield didn't emulate the celebrity culture of his day so much as create it, and he demonstrates the wider point that Christianity was no mere passenger in the making of modernity. "God's dramatist," who could make crowds either laugh or cry by the way he pronounced the word "Mesopotamia"[17] was inevitably accused of gimmickry but one of his signature sermons of the 1740s, *What think ye of Christ?*, suggests the kind of shrewd Enlightenment chemistry that we find in Edwards:

> The Apostle prays that the Ephesians may abound in all knowledge and spiritual understanding, or as it might be rendered, spiritual sensation.... For there is a spiritual, as well as a corporeal feeling; and though this is not communicated to us in a sensible manner, as outward objects affect our senses, yet it is as real as any sensible or visible sensation, and may be as truly felt and discerned by the soul, as any impression from without can be felt by the body. All who are born again of God, know that I lie not.[18]

It is in the second wave of the revival, however, the Second Great Awakening in America and the age of William Wilberforce and Thomas Chalmers in Britain, that witnessed more controversial "synergies" with

16. Noll, *America's God*, 76. Emphasis added.
17. Walsh, "Methodism," 28.
18. George Whitefield, *Sermons on important subjects. With a memoir of the author, by S. Drew [&c.]*, (n.p. 1828), 292.

modern values and attitudes. Nathan Hatch's *The Democratization of American Christianity* (1989) is a vivid account of the "incarnation" of evangelicalism in popular culture during the early life of the Republic: a world of camp meetings, dramatic testimony, and often raucous populism. Antitraditionalism was institutionalized. If Trotsky's idea of the "permanent revolution" had a Christian analogue, this was it. Here was a permanently emerging church in which people's "right . . . to take charge of their own religious destiny" was inalienable, and where roaming preachers such as "Crazy" Lorenzo Dow were idolized. "Public opinion" was exalted "as a primary religious authority,"[19] as Hatch puts it, and a rude, rural culture was Christianized.

Britain did not produce such a heady synthesis of piety and muscle-flexing independence; Christendom was reinvented rather than destroyed, but it was reinvented on terms of competition and choice. Voluntarism replaced parochialism as the accepted basis of Christian affiliation: you chose when and where you went to church. This was no "function" of modernity, but an almost accidental byproduct of revival. Experimental religion demanded freedom of expression, and Wesley's initially reluctant challenge to the parochial network—"I look upon the whole world as my parish"—gained form and substance. The class meetings and Love Feasts of the Methodists, originally a supplement to parochial worship, became its substitutes. "The great invention of evangelicalism was the voluntary society,"[20] writes Callum Brown, and by the mid-nineteenth century, even high churchmen accepted that legal conformity to a given local parish was an impossible ideal. No one quite coined the phrase, "we are all voluntarists now," but T. J. Gaster, the founding vicar of All Saints, Camberwell—the church I now attend—came close: "We are as truly under the 'voluntary system' as the nonconformists are," he wrote in 1896.[21] This was profanity to some, but liberation for others. "Conversionist evangelicalism," writes Brown, "broke the mental chains of the *ancien régime* in Britain. If pre-industrial religiosity stressed individual faith within the context of obedience to church and state, modern evangelicalism laid

---

19. Nathan O. Hatch, *The Democratization of American Christianity* (New Haven: Yale University Press, 1989) 81.

20. Callum G. Brown, *The Death of Christian Britain: Understanding Secularisation 1800–2000* (London: Routledge, 2000), 45.

21. I am grateful to Frog Orr-Ewing, Gaster's successor and my vicar, for this reference.

stress on faith in the context of the individual as a 'free moral agent.' Faith was disjoined from the state by reconceiving religion without the ecclesiastical monopoly of the established churches." "Conversion," as Brown explains, was often described "as 'finding liberty' in a deliberate linguistic evocation of democracy." It was, "no longer something mediated by established churches within a framework of obedience to the state. It became ... the emblem of freedom from the unspiritual state church [as well as] an emblem of renewal within that church. The conversion came to be the most powerful and widely understood symbol of individual freedom in late eighteenth- and nineteenth-century Britain. In a society where equality in political democracy had still a century to run, the equality of the conversion was a powerful notion."[22] Or as John Walsh has written, more simply: "The doctrine of justification by faith alone—free grace—had unexpected resonance among poor people. Its implications were clear: acceptance by God was not dependent, as the poor had often been taught, on the performance of moral duties, on an antecedent life of 'good works' to which ... they could seldom attain."[23]

Modernity is often characterized as an unfortunate accident; something that happens *to* Christianity. The relationship was frequently the other way round, as Christians established norms and values that were later taken up by society at large. Just as the early church has been credited with no less than the "invention of the human" in the brutal world of late antiquity,[24] modern Christians led a revolution in sensibility that counted abolition, infant welfare, and revolutionary notions of equality among its progeny. As John Coffey writes of the struggle to end slavery: "Christian social and political activism has made a major contribution to the culture of modernity."[25] That the dignity of the human agent was later elevated into something we might now dismiss as "individualism" does not challenge the achievement, or its place in the Great Tradition.

The recasting of Christianity as personal, self-authenticating decision was at once disturbing and electrifying. Paul Langford wrote of the episcopal hostility toward the revivalists, which resulted in Methodism's

22. Brown, *Death*, 36, 37.

23. Walsh, "Methodism," 31.

24. See David Bentley Hart, *Atheist Delusions: The Christian Revolution and Its Fashionable Enemies* (New Haven: Yale University Press, 2009) 111ff.

25. John Coffey, "The abolition of the slave trade: Christian conscience and political action." Online: http://www.jubilee-centre.org/document.php?id=51.

formal separation in the 1790s: "The Church, it was increasingly obvious, was ready to amputate an offending limb over which it had no control."[26] Even loyal Anglican Evangelicals struggled to marry their piety to their conformity. Wilberforce had no intention of undermining the Church of England but his *Practical View* (1797), the manifesto of early nineteenth-century evangelicalism, drew a dramatic contrast between "real Christianity" and what he termed "hereditary religion": the oak-aged product of the establishment. The gentle rhythms of Christendom, he suggested, produced a complacency that was unequal to the challenges of the day. As he gently parodied the religion of the typical Englishman: "He was born in a Christian country; of course he is a Christian: his father was a member of the Church of England; so is he. When such is the religion handed down among us by hereditary succession, it cannot surprise us to observe young men of sense and spirit beginning to doubt altogether of the truth of the system in which they have been brought up, and ready to abandon a station which they are unable to defend."[27] Faith had to be personal. It also had to be contemporary.

This is why Wilberforce refused to distance himself from those lay, inter-denominational missionary agencies that many felt to be subverting the Church. The 1820s saw an extended controversy over the Bible Society, condemned by one high churchman for "parcelling out the country into new departments, and erecting a lay eldership in each, to supersede the ministrations of the regular Clergy."[28] Yet it was the laity who effectively evangelized the cities. Following the example of Thomas Chalmers in Glasgow, house-to-house visitation by teams of lay people became the model of urban mission. Women had a vital role, because many people would allow a woman rather than a man into their home, and larger numbers of women volunteered than men. If this was pragmatism, who could fault it?

Some of the monuments of evangelical activism, such as the YMCA, emerged as mere whispers of lay enterprise. The YMCA started as a lunchtime prayer group in a London drapery house in 1844. It was

26. Paul Langford, *A Polite and Commercial People: England, 1727–1783* (Oxford: Oxford University Press, 1989) 270.

27. William Wilberforce, *A practical view of the prevailing religious system of professed Christians, in the higher and middle classes in this country* (n.p. London, 1797; 1834 ed.) 6.

28. Brown, *National Churches*, 59.

said that when the founder, George Williams, entered the business of Hitchcock and Rogers, in the City of London, "it was difficult for any of the hundred and forty assistants to be Christians, within three years . . . it was difficult to be anything else." Williams was a master of man-to-man evangelism and his advice to fellow missionaries—"don't argue with him, invite him to supper"—is strangely contemporary. The YMCA moved from bedroom, to coffeehouse, to hotel, to rented premises on Aldersgate Street. Soon there were branches in every major town or city, and by the 1850s, it was an international movement. Designed as a mid-wife between converts and churches, the YMCA generated powerful loyalties of its own. YMCA members did the work that "the bishops cannot do," boasted one—commending Christ "in the sphere of their daily calling." By 1894 George Williams had received a knighthood and few questioned the status of the lay missionary.[29]

If the coffeeshop and lecture hall ministry of the YMCA was typical of London, the foraging, Monday-to-Sunday activism of Methodism came to dominate the new industrial areas, many of which were beyond Anglican provision altogether. Here, too, there was a sense of symbiosis between the demands of commercial life and the challenges of the Gospel: the perils of temptation, the rewards of industry, the comforts of fellowship. A study of one industrial town found that a disproportionate number of entrepreneurs came from evangelical nonconformist backgrounds, where thrift and independence were the values of the nursery. Evangelical Nonconformity was as central to the new industrial order as Anglicanism was to the so-called *ancien regime*. As W. F. Hook famously observed as newly appointed Vicar of Leeds in 1837: "The *de facto* established religion is Methodism." And as Hempton has written: "The Methodist quarterly [membership] ticket was as much a symbol of the demise of the English confessional state as the Toleration Act of 1812 or the constitutional revolution of 1828–32."[30] A marginal, interstitial movement had become "the church of first resort"—to steal a phrase Rowan Williams has applied to the Church of England. The bad lands of industrialism had been colonized. The "religion of barns" had moved into the square, redbrick chapels that dotted the industrial landscape. Unprepossessing and often ugly, they

---

29. For more on the YMCA, see Dominic Erdozain, *The Problem of Pleasure: Sport, Recreation and the Crisis of Victorian Religion* (Woodbridge, UK: Boydell, 2010).

30. David Hempton, *The Religion of the People: Methodism and Popular Religion, C.1750–1900* (London: Routledge, 1996) 26.

were, as the Congregationalist R.W. Dale later put it, "the visible symbols of a faith which was unconscious of things seen and temporal."[31]

The church's initial response was simply to build more churches, but they rarely filled up, and almost never with the poor. As a character in one of Charles Kingsley's novels reflected: "After all the expense, when they've built the church, it's the tradesmen and the gentry and the old folk that fill it, and the working men never come near it from one year's end to another."[32] The church was still handicapped by a sense of entitlement to the affections of the people. It was seemingly oblivious of the effects of its association with "the old order," or what radicals termed "the old corruption." The centrality of the Church of England to a political and judicial system that had to be dragged, kicking and screaming, into reform in the 1830s was enduringly damaging. It took broad churchmen of socialist sympathies such as Kingsley and F. D. Maurice to grasp what evangelical Nonconformists sensed intuitively: the church needed to be less elitist, less rigidly formal, even less church-like in order to reach the people. The message hit home after the traumas of the parliamentary Reform Bill crisis, when the bishops' opposition in the House of Lords brought the country "within an ace of a revolution."[33] Suddenly, clerics like Kingsley were on the streets, circulating their ideas through fiction rather than sermons, and claiming museums and galleries among the agents of Christian grace. Evangelical Anglicans caught the mood and started to mingle sacred and secular as never before. Anglican places of worship listed in the 1851 census returns for my own parish of Camberwell included Peckham police station, Dulwich College, and a Licensed Victuallers Asylum. Out of twelve places of worship, only five were what you would call "churches." This was in addition to several Nonconformist gatherings. Religious provision was chaotic but effective. The methods of the revival were permeating the establishment.

If hypocrisy is the compliment vice pays to virtue, respectability was the inevitable byproduct of popularity. The pride of aristocratic privilege had been punctured, but who was to say that the more populist successor

---

31. Robert William Dale, *The Evangelical Revival, and Other Sermons* (London: Hodder & Stoughton, 1880) 27.

32. Quoted in K. S. Inglis, *Churches and the Working Classes in Victorian England* (New York: Routledge, 1973) 18.

33. E. P. Thompson, *The Making of the English Working Class* (London: Vintage, 1980) 817.

would be immune to the vices of ease and acculturation? The 1850s and 1860s were the start of what one historian of Methodism has termed "our mahogany age"—the age of respect and respectability: "We got our mahogany pulpits and the preachers found their way to the mahogany tables of wealthy laymen."[34] Female and open-air preaching had been banned in 1803 but it was not until much later that a sense of denominational stasis settled on the movement as a whole. Yet, again, we witness the centrifugal power of evangelical zeal. Just when the Victorian ideology of "separate spheres" was fixing the boundaries of female conduct with unyielding precision, preachers such as Ann Swailes broke them. Swailes was a Primitive Methodist whose "sorrow" for the "thousands of souls perishing" led her inexorably into preaching. Her position hardened in the thickening air of reproach: "Tell me it is wrong for a woman to preach and I will say it is right," she protested, "God has told me hundreds of times. If a man was drowning and a female threw the rope, would he not seize it to save his life because it was female?"[35] If evangelicalism was marked by "an aversion to systems and metaphysics, a preference for clarity and simplicity,"[36] this was purest evangelicalism. Catherine Booth and the Salvation Army later built upon the same principle.

A final example is Charles Spurgeon, the boy wonder who gathered his first congregation at age nineteen, and raised eyebrows in 1856 by moving it to the largest and most notorious music hall in London, while his new church was being built. Evangelicals had been fighting a turf war against the theatres, music halls, and a range of popular sports for decades, so it was a matter of consternation when this irreverent, almost uncouth, young preacher decided to conduct services in the Surrey Gardens Music Hall. Spurgeon saw no contradiction in bringing the Gospel to the very sites of irreligion and, in 1857, he accepted an invitation to preach at the Crystal Palace, the enormous glass exhibition center in south London, which had been at the center of a bitter struggle over Sunday opening. Regarded by some as a "Temple of Belial," a den of "rampant pleasure," Spurgeon's decision to preach there was controversial. But as liberal

---

34. Inglis, *Churches*, 85.

35. Linda Wilson, "'Constrained by Zeal': Women in Mid-Nineteenth Century Nonconformist Churches," *Journal of Religious History* 23:2 (1999) 200.

36. Bebbington, "Response," in *The Emergence of Evangelicalism: Exploring Historical Continuities*, eds. Michael A. G. Haykin and Kenneth J. Stewart (Nottingham: InterVarsity, 2008) 426.

commentators wryly observed, his presence alone cast doubt on the notion that God automatically punishes Sabbath breakers. His elegant sermon on the verse, "Behold the Lamb of God," was heard by twenty-four thousand people. A taboo had been shattered. A similar event was organized at Epsom Racecourse, another nerve-center of indignation, where he spoke from the grandstand. "So run that ye may obtain," was his text.[37] Dismissed as a showman and celebrity, it is fair to say that the world embraced Spurgeon before the religious world did. In 1870, *Vanity Fair* featured him as one of their "Men of the Day," a smiter of Philistines and a defier of convention. *"No one has succeeded like him in sketching the comic side of repentance and regeneration,"* gushed the editor. Again: a radical ministry that, by the 1880s, had become a model of orthodoxy. Humor in the pulpit was virtually Spurgeon's invention, and his informal style, which included non-clerical dressing and a preference for "Mr." rather than "Reverend" sparked a host of imitators. It is strange to see him, popping up on the blogs, as a timeless rebuke to contemporary culture gazing. When the emerging church is condemned for allowing Christians to continue "drinking, smoking, [and] indulging in the culture that leads them away from God,"[38] I am reminded of Spurgeon's response when he was challenged for smoking a pipe: he smoked it, he said, "to the glory of God." And, far from condemning alcohol, he actually regarded teetotalism, with its confidence in the powers of the human will, as the greater enemy of the Gospel. Asked to preach on teetotalism in the 1850s, he said he would rather "lay the axe at the root of the tree" than speak in favor of it.[39] He later changed his mind about drink, but this was no hidebound Puritan.

How, then, did matters unravel? Where did the permanent ecclesiological revolution come unstuck? The short answer is that the cultural environment was elevated from the context of Christian mission to the primary text. The city and its supposedly unique challenges gained the casting vote in matters of mission and ecclesiology. The evangelical virtues

37. Rosemary Chadwick, "Spurgeon, Charles Haddon (1834–1892)," in *Oxford Dictionary of National Biography*, eds. H. C. G. Matthew and Brian Harrison (Oxford: Oxford University Press, 2004). Online: http://www.oxforddnb.com/view/article/26187.

38. Andy Rowell, comment on "The Emerging Church," Christianity Today Live Blog, comment posted April 3, 2009. Online: http://blog.christianitytoday.com/ctliveblog/archives/2009/04/the_emerging_ch.html.

39. William Williams, *Personal Reminiscences of Charles Haddon Spurgeon* (London: Religious Tract Society, 1895) 39.

of attentiveness and flexibility became liabilities. There was no sudden crisis: rather, a gradual mutation of the Christian mission into a thousand sub-ministries which, in the twentieth century, could be performed as well—if not better—by secular specialists. The 1880s and 1890s were the crucial decades, dominated by figures such as the Methodist Hugh Price Hughes and the Congregationalist Charles Sylvester Horne. Claiming a robust if unangular orthodoxy, their habit was to set Christian practice against the hollowness of mere belief. We are as orthodox as our fathers, they would say, but we have no time for the finer points of doctrine: there is a world to be healed! And the world had moved on. Innovation went from a natural response to new conditions to a self-conscious preoccupation. The ingenuous spontaneity of former years gave way to statistics, tables, and an almost managerial activism.[40]

Few of the new generation denied the need for personal salvation, but they de-emphasized it in favor of a broader notion of redemption, encompassing the body as well as the soul, and society as well as the individual. Revivalism was disdained. Otherworldliness was out. Charles Sylvester Horne impressed audiences by praying with his eyes wide open; Hugh Price Hughes made a point of quoting from risqué magazines, such as *Punch*. But this was about more than just style: Hughes launched a "Forward Movement" in 1885, the whole tenor of which was a rebuke to evangelical narrowness. In an address to a packed YMCA meeting at the Albert Hall in 1893, Hughes derided the limitations of "their fathers, who were other-worldly, and more concerned about their own souls." "This was an age of practical Christianity," he asserted, and it was time for Christians to "prove their loyalty to Jesus Christ by helping to stamp out the evils of our day." There was "Gambling . . . the cause of purity in India . . . [and] The question of war, too, should be dealt with . . . these were the kind of subjects [Christian organizations] must deal with, if [they] hoped to flourish in the 20th Century." Hughes was heckled as he urged the YMCA to support the campaign for prohibition. "It's not political," insisted the heckler. Hughes responded by saying that "if the YMCA was not political in that sense, then it did not represent Jesus Christ."[41] Hughes

---

40. For a more detailed account of the argument presented in the following paragraphs, see Dominic Erdozain, *The Problem of Pleasure: Sport, Recreation and the Crisis of Victorian Religion* (Woodbridge, UK: Boydell, 2010).

41. National Council of the Young Men's Christian Association, Annual Report, 1893, 18.

was no liberal. He experienced a classic conversion as a teenager and was not someone haunted by hermeneutics of suspicion. Yet he increasingly allowed his political and ethical preoccupations to define orthodoxy. "The times" and their unique challenges set the Christian agenda.

The pressure of Christian obligation gradually shifted until faith and creed were eclipsed by campaign and action. The creedal contents seemed to drop out without anyone noticing. Far from a holistic, integrated theology balancing the atonement with the incarnation, the emerging model was specialist, divisive, and effectively inverted evangelical soteriology. Rather than seeing sin as spiritual and needing a supernatural "cure," the hands-on mentality had the effect of "physicalizing" it as a set of tangible urban problems, mostly revolving around drink. Holiness was redefined as a form of manly self-possession, fuelled by sociological analysis that suggested the irrelevance of intellectual approaches. It was recognized that alienation from the churches was rarely caused by atheism, so, the argument went, people needed to be drawn back socially, with a minimum of complicating doctrine. Whereas Spurgeon had colonized the sites of popular leisure, interrupting their logic even as he borrowed their idiom, the new idea was to sail more boldly with the cultural wind. Dynamic encounter evolved into naïve appropriation. All that was exciting, popular or manly was to be emulated. The flagship was the so-called "Pleasant Sunday Afternoon" or PSA movement that launched in the 1880s to capture the elusive working-class male. PSAs were exciting, informal services, organized under the slogan, "brief, bright and brotherly." Horne called it a "New Protestantism." "The words 'PSA,'" writes one historian, "symbolized all that was original and fresh in [late-Victorian Christianity]."[42] Perhaps so, but trivialization and a vagueness of Christian purpose haunted the PSA from the start. In 1891 the *Free Methodist* published the following "Hearty Invitation" to a PSA in West Hartlepool:

> Tonight Mr. Fred Hunter, the noted tenor, of Hartlepool, Miss Kirkup (soprano) and Miss Miller (contralto) will sing. Mr. Wheatley will play a violin solo. A good choir will render a couple of grand choruses from Handel or other great composer; and Rev. J. Longden will say two or three plain things about "Rogues, thieves, and vagabonds." Just an hour—from seven to eight o'clock. You can

---

42. Hugh McLeod, *Class and Religion in the Late Victorian City* (London: Croom Helm, 1974), 65.

sit where you like, go in where you like, and come out where you like. There's no collection, and a sheet of hymns for everybody.[43]

Another PSA enthusiast invited his congregation to spit on the floor if it was their custom. The openness and generosity cannot be faulted, but the step from recognizing the dangers of too much theology to forgetting it yourself was short and easily taken. Many sources of this period evoke the sense that theology was yesterday's luxury. "I act, therefore I am" was the unofficial motto of the late-Victorian churches. The suggestion that Christ may have been uneasy about the new practicality caused one Christian teetotaler to respond that, "Christ . . . did not live in Shoreditch in the nineteenth century." In 1892, a high-profile Christian journalist explained his refusal to speak on the subject of Melchizedek and the priestly order: "You have round you drunkenness, lust, oppression; Melchizedek may wait till you have got rid of these!"[44] Circumstances were no longer respected: they were obeyed.

Like a business carving up a target market, Victorian Christians divided and subdivided the religious problem by age, gender, class, and occupation until there were niche ministries for almost everyone. Texts such as *Tempted London* (1888), out of the same stable as W. T. Stead's *If Christ Came to Chicago* (1894), mapped the spiritual problem with street-by-street precision. Mission was defined by a mixture of social theology, statistics, and the "new journalism" of scandal and exposure, of which Stead was the master. Suddenly we find YMCAs measuring their success not in converts but in the numbers of people who had used their facilities and the victory over "vice" that this apparently represented. Debates centered on the minutiae of opening hours and the proximity of branches to music halls. The statistics of drinking, gambling, and prostitution were the reference point. People wrote to thank the YMCA for "saving" them from the urban morass, employing the vocabulary of evangelical conviction with only passing reference to faith or God. Salvation was being secularized as health, manliness—virtue.

Meanwhile, churches reorganized under the "institutional principle." Institutional churches provided an umbrella for a medley of clubs, agencies, and services, aiming to unite them under a common Christian ethos. But it never quite worked. The damning statistic was that, in the

---

43. Quoted in Erdozain, *Problem of Pleasure*, 196.
44. *British Weekly* (March 31, 1892), 365.

1880s and 90s, parachurch agencies were rapidly outstripping church membership. The Wesleyan Methodists discovered in 1888 that while their agencies were set to double within twenty years, full church membership would take a hundred years. More and more people were passing through their doors but fewer of them were engaging with the worshipping center of the churches. An official report blamed the "ecclesiastical machinery"[45] that now dominated their institutions: "church" now meant too many different things. Congregationalists similarly complained that weekday activities and meetings had become competitors to prayer meetings. Gymnasiums, men's clubs, and the cult of clean living did not prove to be a gateway to spirituality: too often they provided a way *out* of serious commitment. Even when this was not the case, William Gladstone's critique of evangelical ecclesiology rang true. Evangelicals, the statesman and high churchman argued, tended to evince "more Churchmanship, more inward sense of the personal obligations entailed by belonging to a given religious society" than in the church as such. The result was often clusters of like-minded believers working on specific causes, and little of that involuntary unity that true discipleship requires. "Individualism in religion," he wrote, was "their besetting weakness."[46]

Specialism and activism were therefore increasingly under attack. "We seem likely to place every one of the Ten Commandments under the protection of a separate Committee, with its Treasurer, Secretary, and deputations, and to organise a League for the promotion of every separate grace," complained R. W. Dale in 1880. A census of London's mission halls in 1888 highlighted the issues. As the editor of the leading evangelical newspaper, the *British Weekly*, reflected: "We frankly confess to being surprised, disappointed, and perplexed by the results. The whole question of new methods in religion is most seriously raised by this census."[47] The disappointment was not merely with the small numbers reached by these agencies but the fact that many who attended them were already churchgoers. PSAs were simply drawing people from other congregations. One writer complained that ministers were being "bustled out of their spirituality"[48] by the new ecclesiology. Others argued that, even when successful, the model of

---

45. *Report of the Proceedings of the Committee on Church-Membership* (London, 1888), Appendix, 15.
46. Dale, *Revival*, 30–31.
47. *British Weekly* (January 13, 1888) 201.
48. *British Weekly* (December 31, 1891) 158.

tailored, targeted ministries was unbiblical. Churches seemed to be endorsing the status quo even as they grappled with it.

William Cuff, a Baptist whose preaching attracted London's third largest congregation, the Shoreditch Tabernacle, used the census to attack the "caste" mentality embodied in "the mad-brained passion for mission halls." He resented the suggestion that only the Salvation Army, with its aggressive populism, could really engage the poor. His church flourished with a strict membership policy and none of the aped merriment of the music halls. Archibald Brown, another box-office Baptist from the East End, produced a pamphlet in 1889 entitled *The Devil's Mission of Amusement*. He suggested that the spirit of 1 Corinthians 9:22: "I am made all things to all men . . ." had been abused. "Modern methods" were dissolving the Gospel more profoundly than "modern thought." "Success" in Christian work was being defined as keeping people out of the music halls: a lean victory if you turn church into a music hall. A culture of accessibility and openness had now entered "into competition" with the Gospel. The "sanctuary" had to be restored.[49]

Meanwhile, the Congregationalists, who had been at the cutting edge of the new ecclesiology, suddenly recoiled from its implications. As the Congregational Union chairman reflected in 1891: "The [modern] idea is that the Church needs supplementing in its own domain by a host of collateral little states. Our polity means a *Church*, it does not mean a cluster of institutions. Many of our Churches are very busy at the present time in the formation of societies to supersede themselves. We must not let the Church idea be crowded out by the multiplicity of our organizations . . . ."[50] Contemporary wisdom held that any Christian gathering is as sacred as another, that the fellowship of the cricket club was as sacred as that of the church proper, but this speaker urged: "As you exalt the one, is it not—if we may not say inevitable—at any rate highly probable that you depress the other?" The same was true of doctrine: "The insistence upon the introduction of the secular element into our church life . . . has this effect—that actually, though perhaps not logically, *it remits theology, including doctrinal teaching, to a subordinate place, and often to entire extinction.*"[51] Lines had to be drawn. Christianity is not a matter of rules and fences, argued one, but fences have their place.

49. Erdozain, *Problem of Pleasure*, 235ff.
50. *Congregational Year Book* (1891) 70.
51. Ibid., 62.

The *British Weekly* argued similarly in a major, stocktaking article entitled, "Why Orthodox Men Do Not Preach the Gospel." The current tendency was to hold back "what is astonishing in Christianity," to major on the ethical at the expense of the spiritual, and to keep the old language of conversion for emergencies. This was secularization by occlusion not denial, and it presages aspects of what Brueggemann and Walker have termed gospel "amnesia."[52] P. T. Forsyth, the great Congregationalist theologian, observed it first hand. He argued that Evangelical Nonconformity had, by the first decade of the twentieth century, drifted into a culture of "sympathy." And, as he thundered, "Sympathy is not adequate to redeem." Theology had descended into "a branch of journalism" and the resulting ecclesiology was an attempt to reform society "by every benevolent means except the evangelical." "The agencies have become of more interest than the Communion," he lamented, and they "represent[ed] an itch of activity rather than [true] Christian energy." They would not last. Forsyth was not above exaggeration, but he grasped the ambiguity of a culture-saturating revival that had started to "go native":

> Culture, aesthetic or even religious [he wrote in 1896] is now the most deadly and subtle enemy of spiritual freedom. It is the growth of culture in the decay of Gospel that the soul's freedom has increasingly to dread. It is there that our Nonconformity is in most danger of being untrue to itself and its mission. We *are* suffering. But it is less from grievance now than from success. We share a prosperity which is passing through variety of interest, refinement of taste, aesthetic emotion, tender pity, kindly careless catholicity, and over-sweet reasonableness, to leanness of soul. It is more at home in literature than in Scripture, and in journals more than either. And it tends to substitute charity and its sympathies for grace and its faith. These are tendencies of the time which we have not escaped . . . . Humanism must indeed find a home in grace which it has never occupied yet. *But it is another thing when it becomes a church's note.*[53]

Such warnings may have been too late for a British tradition that avoided the polarities of the liberal-fundamentalist divide by occupying a middle ground of ethical toil. There were, however, those who heeded

---

52. Andrew Walker, *Telling the Story: Gospel, Mission and Culture*, Gospel and Culture Series (London: SPCK, 1996) 48; Walker is quoting Walter Brueggemann.

53. Peter Taylor Forsyth, *The Charter of the Church. Six Lectures on the Spiritual Principle of Nonconformity* (London: Alexander & Shepheard, 1896) v.

the call to a sharpened ecclesiology, and were even willing to take lessons from the Catholics. Peace broke out in some of the leading journals—the *British Weekly* offering the startling observation that the "High Church" was not "popular for satisfying a low craving for sensuous worship," as per standard evangelical prejudice, but "for insisting on the great elementary facts of Christianity."[54] Dogma and liturgy had their place. Alexander MacLaren used his chairman's address to the Baptist Union in 1901 to appeal for "Evangelical Mysticism." "Martha has it all her own way now," was his evocative analysis: it was time to re-learn the harder discipline of "sitting at Jesus' feet in blessed receptivity." "Life is the root of work," he urged, and "is more important than work." "The Christian activities of this day specially need the deepening consecration of the Mystical side of [the Christian faith]." A generation reared on a tail-chasing activism needed to hear three simple words: "Abide in Me."[55] A more famous example is the hunger for sacrament evoked by soldiers in the First World War. Army chaplains started the war handing out cigarettes and bonhomie; they ended it distributing the Eucharist. It took war to demonstrate just how humanistic and earthbound even "orthodoxy" had become: there was a new yearning for mystery, transcendence, and spiritual solace.

Finally, among the exhausted testimonies recorded in Charles Booth's *Life and Labour of the People in London* (1902) was the account of a ministry transformed by renouncing the cult of comprehensiveness and relearning the habits of prayer, catechism, and discipline. The report came from an unnamed Anglican mission, where the minister had become exasperated with the leisure-based methods with which he had started. Local residents constantly assured him that they were members of the mission when, in fact, they went there to play billiards or drink tea. As he explained, the evangelistic gateway had become its own barrier to the gospel:

> When I came to the mission, I had the very strongest hopes with regard to a kind of social work, reaching the people through all sorts of channels—one would not trouble much about anything else if only the people were "reached." Experience brings a stern schooling, but a very convincing one . . . . Three main principles gradually came out clear—(i) Anything that was merely popular in order to attract masses of people, without the mark of sacrifice

---

54. *British Weekly* (February 5, 1891) 238.
55. *Baptist Hand-Book* (1902) 124–25.

on it, to be sternly repressed. (ii) To build on a clear and definite religious basis, made intelligible to the people by constant teaching. (iii) To loyally carry out every part of the Prayer Book in the daily life of the people.[56]

Having abandoned the earlier strategy, he was "more and more convinced that the truest way to help those we long to reach, is by having the standard a high one, and not a low one." It was "a mistake to 'come down to their level.'" Initially there might be a thinning of numbers, "but it is only for the moment while the seed is being sown. Very soon the intensity of the work tells." "There must be intensity before extension" was the new principle: "Instead of lowering the standard by popular attractions, throw your whole available time into unsparing training of your small body of people, and [only then seek] the multitude . . . . Sooner or later [people] would be reached . . . their respect for Religion would have grown as they saw its seriousness, its sacrifice, its true and definite mark of the Cross, instead of mere popular attractiveness." The "men's club" had been reconstituted so that it was now "assumed, as a natural thing, that those who belong to the club shall come to church." Several other agencies "which seemed to be isolated from the church" had been integrated by a stricter membership policy and a system of "catechizing." The Book of Common Prayer had become, once again, "*common* prayer." He felt "bound to bear testimony to its unique power and hold among the very poorest."[57] Like a venerable musician rediscovering the tunes that had made her famous, such ministries went back to basics, recovering a distinction between the sources of Christian faith and mere modes of expression. Context, it seemed, was not everything. There was a dogmatic core that needed to be rescued from layers of contemporary packaging.

Religious traditions, no less than nations, are "imagined communities."[58] How they perceive history is a real factor in their life and progress. In the twentieth century, many Christians were paralyzed by the "secularization thesis" and its promise of inevitable decline. Dwindling churches were occasionally closed down because, in someone's mind, "the trends" were "irreversible." A danger now is that Christians are mesmer-

56. Charles Booth, *Life and Labour of the People in London* (London: Macmillan, 1902) 3rd series, Religious Influences, 7:91–93.

57. Ibid., 93.

58 Frank M. Turner, *John Henry Newman: The Challenge to Evangelical Religion* (New Haven, CT: Yale University Press, 2002) 43.

ized by "postmodernity," and share a fashionable, ahistorical scorn for "the Enlightenment project" and its progeny. There are good reasons to question the ethos of modernity and its exaltation of human choice, but the awkward fact is that, without it, Christianity may never have broken out of a hierarchical and desiccated Christendom of the early-modern era. The evangelical movement was indeed "a child of the Enlightenment,"[59] and if it took on some of the vices of the parent it also inherited virtues. The faith in formulae, techniques, and statistics may now repel but such things were no more the essence of the modern than David's sin of "numbering Israel"[60] was a function of pre-exilic Israel. Evangelical innovations were not wanton dalliances with a thinly disguised paganism: doomed from the outset. John Milbank's dismissal of Chalmers' synthesis of theology and political economy as "a mean little heresy"[61] displays the arrogance that can flow from a sense of having grown out of the adolescent infatuations of the modern. What are *our* heresies? People like Chalmers may have been too quick to associate the "invisible hand" with God, but they used the drama of the economy, just as Edwards used the kindling of Enlightenment philosophy, to reignite the Christian imagination. If individualism was a heresy, "it is," as William Temple once wrote, "worthwhile to notice how absolute was Christ's respect for the freedom of personal choice. He would neither bribe nor coerce men to become his followers."[62] Evangelicals reminded Christendom of this irreducible fact, and if they contributed to the dismantling of Christendom in working it out, there were both positive and negative implications. Their strength was to be unfazed by giddying cultural change; their weakness was to be molded by it. Both legacies are part of that living stream of wisdom and folly, grace and leaden human error, that we term the Great Tradition.

---

59. Gary J. Williams characterising Bebbington's thesis, "Enlightenment Epistemology and Eighteenth-Century Evangelical Doctrines of Assurance," in *The Emergence of Evangelicalism: Exploring Historical Continuities*, eds. Michael A. G. Haykin and Kenneth H. Stewart (Nottingham: InterVarsity, 2008) 347.

60. 1 Chron 21:1.

61. John Milbank, *Theology and Social Theory: Beyond Secular Reason*, 1st ed. (Oxford: Blackwell, 1990) 45.

62. William Temple, *Christianity and Social Order* (London: Shepheard-Walwyn, 1976) 69.

www.ingramcontent.com/pod-product-compliance
Lightning Source LLC
Chambersburg PA
CBHW032233080426
42735CB00008B/832